GAS GRILL COOKBOOK FOR BEGINNERS

Quick and Easy Grill Recipes to Make Delicious and Healthy Food With Illustrated Recipes. Master Grilled Food for Everyday Meals and the Whole Family.

Table of Contents

CHAPTER 4. MEAT RECIPES BURGER, STEAKS, LAMB, BEEF, POULTRY, GAME, AND PORK 22

INTRODUCTION

The gas grill is a special variant of the grill and is operated in most cases with butane gas. Compared to the charcoal grill, the gas grill has some decisive advantages, because it is much easier to ignite and enables the food to be prepared more gently. In addition, there is significantly less smoke and smell, which is particularly pleasing to the neighbors, as they no longer feel annoyed. Also, the gas grill can not only be used in your own garden, it is also wonderful to use on the terrace or even the balcony.

The gas grill usually has a hood that is not only closed for heating, but also for cooking. The hood is made of the same material as the rest of the grill and is weatherproof. At the front of the hood, there is usually a handle that does not get hot, so the hood can be opened at any time to look at the food to be grilled. Robust stainless steel or cast iron is often used for production, as these materials are characterized by their high-quality workmanship. They are independent of the weather and can therefore be left outside without problems.

To be able to move the gas grill as desired, it is partly equipped with practical castors. The gas grill can be moved to easily change the position for grilling if necessary. The effort required is very low, so there is a high degrees of flexibility. In addition to the rollers, most models have storage options on the sides for the grill accessories, which can be folded up and down if necessary.

The advantage over a charcoal grill is that the grill temperature can be set individually. In this way, the heat levels can be perfectly adapted to the food to be grilled to achieve an optimized cooking point. For this purpose, there are usually handy rotary knobs in the front area, which can be regulated accordingly. This means that many different foods can be prepared on the gas grill without something burning or overcooking.

The gas grill is equipped with a special valve that regulates the gas supply air. As soon as the gas bottle has been connected, the gas tap is turned on in order to be able to ignite the grill. The gas cylinder is available in different sizes so that it can be perfectly adapted to your own needs. As a rule, one gas bottle is sufficient for several barbecues, depending on how long it has been in use. Most gas grills are equipped with a small compartment below the grill surface, where the gas bottle can be placed without it being immediately visible. In the case of smaller models, however, it is usually placed directly next to it.

The gas then flows into the pipe system, which is located under the grate. The grill grate offers enough space to place meat, fish, or vegetables on it. The gas supply can now be regulated using the rotary knobs, i.e., the heat can be adjusted to the food being grilled. In contrast to a charcoal grill, which often has a long lighting time, the gas grill is ready for use after around five to ten minutes.

What Can It Do?

CHAPTER 1.
EVERYTHING YOU
NEED TO KNOW
ABOUT A GAS GRILL

Cleaning and Care of the Gas Grill

Before you can start cleaning the gas grill, there are a few things to consider. First and foremost, you must bring the right tools with you to be able to carry out cleaning at all. This includes, for example:

- A grill brush
- A rag
- A bucket of warm water
- Cleaner and care products

First, the grease drip tray should be emptied. A lot of dirt accumulates when cleaning, because dirt and liquids run into the grease trap, so it is quickly overflowed.

Burning out the gas grill is known as pyrolysis and it kills any organic residue in the grill. Food scraps, fats, and organic residues burn, leaving nothing but pure carbon that can be easily removed. After the burnout, the actual cleaning takes place. The interior is divided into three sections:

1. The cooking grids
2. The grill lid
3. The combustion chamber

The grill grates are easily cleaned with the brush. This means that soot and suspended matter can be easily removed. It is then advisable to rub the grate with a little oil or spray it with a grease spray.

The lid can usually be cleaned easily with a little warm water, a little washing-up liquid, and a cloth. A special grill cleaner can also be used for heavier soiling so that the lid looks like new again in the end. It is important that a biological grill cleaner is used, as chemical additives can harm the food during preparation.

Now the combustion chamber remains, which of course also has to be cleaned. To do this, the gas bottle and grill grates need to be removed. The flame trays can be removed and worked with a brush. This also applies to the combustion chamber itself, the encrustations and dirt of which can usually only be removed with a brush. Finally, the whole thing is washed out again with clear water and a damp cloth so that the gas grill is ready for the next grill session.

Finally, let's take a look at the outside area of the gas grill. Basically, the outside of the gas grill doesn't need much attention, but regular cleaning is important so that it looks and lasts for a long time. The surfaces of the gas grill can be properly lathered with water and washing-up liquid and washed off. If, on the other hand, it is heavier soiling, a grill cleaner can also be used to loosen the soiling. Anyone who leaves the gas grill outside during the year should definitely think about a cover. In this way, it remains protected from rain and snow and is not directly exposed to the weather conditions.

Advantages of a Gas Grill at a Glance

- 5 to 10 minutes to the right temperature
- The gas bottle is enough for several barbecues
- Start possible at the push of a button
- Temperature control via a rotary knob
- Suitable for meat, fish, chicken, and vegetables
- With shelf
- Optionally with stove top
- Healthy grilling
- Hardly any smoke or odor development
- Also suitable for balcony use
- Plenty of accessories available
- Cools down quickly
- Easy to clean

Disadvantages of a Gas Grill at a Glance

- The gas bottle must be bought or borrowed
- The purchase price of the gas grill can be very expensive
- Some accessories have to be purchased separately

How Safe Is a Gas Grill?

Gas grills can be a great way to get yourself cooking outdoors and enjoying the summer weather. But how safe is a gas grill?

The National Fire Protection Association (NFPA) says that gas grills are about 100 times less likely to cause fires than other kinds, like charcoal grills. That's because gas burns more cleanly than other fuels and doesn't create an open flame that's liable to start a brushfire or flare-up.

So if you have a gas grill, don't worry too much about it being a fire hazard. But gas grills can be dangerous in other ways—like if they tip over.

How to Start a Gas Grill?

Gas grills are great because you don't have to deal with the hassle or mess of using charcoal. Plus, they can be easier to control and more fuel-efficient than other types of grills. However, they need a little more understanding to get them going safely and efficiently every time. Luckily for you, we are here with just that!

We have all the information you need on how to start your gas grill, including how long it will take for a gas grill vs a charcoal grill cooking times! Follow our instructions below and your next cookout will be a total hit!

1. Screw-in the gas line connector by hand or use a wrench if necessary. The connector should be screwed in firmly, but not too tight. Tighten it clockwise. Never use force if it does not unscrew—you could ruin the connector or even damage your grill.

2. Check to see that gas is coming out of the valve and watch for a steady stream. If the stream is intermittent, open and close the valve several times to clear any air out of the line. Wait about 5 minutes before proceeding to Step 3 to allow gas time to travel through your grill lines and into your tank. A new tank will take longer than an empty one—up to 15 minutes—so plan for this when lighting your grill, especially on a cold day when warm-up time can take longer as well.

3. Preheat the grill on medium heat. Once it reaches 500 °F (260 °C) , light the main burner or burners you want to use. The high heat should help the grill ignite the gas line.

4. If you are using an open grill, close the lid. If you are using a cover, remove it now so that it doesn't get in the way of ignition. You will need to clean your grill after every use so that any residue will be burned off and that there is enough space for all sides of your grill to warm up properly before cooking begins.

5. Once you have a steady blue or blue-white flame, adjust the burner to bring the heat down to a lower setting.

6. Leave the grill unattended—never try to re-light a gas grill!—and enjoy your delicious food!

The Difference between Charcoal and Gas Grill

A gas grill will typically have 5 burners, with 4 being covered and one being used for ignition purposes. They also require time for the tank to warm up so that all of the burners come on at once. An average gas grill will take about 40 minutes to preheat.

A charcoal grill is a little different because it will not be as efficient as a gas grill. You can expect it to take around 10 minutes to preheat on medium heat. However, charcoal can be made more efficient by building up the charcoal layer and stirring them before cooking with them.

Mistakes to Avoid When Using a Gas Grill

- Don't use a propane tank that is more than a year old.
- Make sure you buy the correct size propane tank for your grill. Smaller tanks are only good for cooking out for 1 hour or less, while larger tanks can cook out for 4 hours or more at a time.
- Don't overfill your propane tank. Extra gas is harmful to the environment and creates useless weight on top of your tank! Remember, though, that too little propane could result in a flame that goes out too soon, making it harder to cook. Make sure to fill until you see 2 inches (5,1 cm) of space between the top of the propane and the top of the tank.
- To make sure your tank is filled correctly, check the owner's manual or look for indicators on the tank itself. The pressure release valve should be facing up, away from the propane tank.
- Don't remove the gas tank until you are actually ready to use it. When storing your grill, make sure that the propane tank is properly secured.

The Right Gas

You're almost ready to start cooking! But before you do, make sure that you are using the right kind of gas. Propane is the most common form of gas used for grills, but it isn't the only one out there! If you are new to grilling or trying something new, consider using a grill with natural gas. Natural gas grills include propane tanks as well as hooks for natural gas hookups.

Make sure that whichever type of grill you're using is compatible with the type of tank that you have chosen. For example, a propane tank will not work on a grill that accepts natural gas tanks.

Direct Grilling Method

When you're grilling with gas, your cooking time will be faster than it would be on a charcoal grill. However, this is because gas grills often use a direct grilling method. This method cooks by using the heat directly underneath the food and ensures that your food comes out fully cooked and tasty every time!

Using this method does not mean that you lose out on flavor! Add some oil to your food before placing it on the grill and the direct flavor of the flame will infuse your food with wonderful flavors as it cooks through.

If you're planning to use this method for cooking, then preheat your grill to 500 °F (260 °C) before adding any food.

Indirect Grilling Method

If this is your first time grilling with gas, then you might want to start off with the indirect grilling method. Cooking this way allows you to use the indirect heat of the grill while still maintaining some flavor.

Indirect methods are usually used for more delicate meats, such as fish, which would not be suitable for direct grilling. This method also cooks food more slowly than direct methods, allowing it to soak in more of the flavor that comes from the grill!

To use an indirect gas grill, leave one or more burners off. Preheat your grill on medium heat and then add your food on the side of the grill that doesn't have any flames underneath it.

The Right Size of the Gas Grill

When it comes to choosing the right size of your gas grill, there are many factors to consider.

Make sure that you buy a grill that is large enough for your needs! You want to be able to cook food for an entire family or even multiple families. If you're just grilling for yourself, then you can choose a smaller grill. The size of your grill is measured in square feet, which refers to the total amount of floor space available in your grill when cooking out. This is usually measured by multiplying the length of the grill in feet by the width of the grill in feet and then dividing that into 144 inches (365,8 cm) .

Where you choose to store your grill is also important. If it isn't going to be stored in a garage or in its own storage space, then you need to make sure that the area where you choose to store your grill will be able to handle the weight of the unit. A larger unit may need multiple people to move it safely!

Weight of the Gas Grill

When you're choosing the right size of your gas grill, make sure that you don't forget the weight! Generally, larger grills are heavier than smaller units. But remember that it is safer to move a lighter grill than to attempt moving one that is too heavy.

Consider the weight of your grill when choosing where to place it for storage! You can damage or break flooring or furniture if you place your grill on an uneven surface.

Watch out for the legs of your gas grill when carrying it! They may look strong enough to hold up the weight, but overextending them could cause them to break if they aren't properly supported by the ground beneath them.

What Should Be Considered When Buying a Gas Grill?

Buying a gas grill is not just about the price. There are many other factors that you need to consider when buying a gas grill.

It's better to buy a gas grill that has good reviews from customers, so read up on the features of the unit before buying it.

Also, check if it has an electric starter before you buy it! If you have an older unit, then it might be hard to get the hot fire going. A newer model may come with an electric starting system so that you can always have your food cooking right away!

Before the First Use

There are some things that it is best to do when buying a gas grill.

Before you take it out of the box, be sure to check if there aren't any small parts that may fall off. Open the package carefully so that you don't damage your unit during transportation. Leave everything out in its original box, so that if it does have any damage, you can return the damaged items to the store.

Always make sure that you have all of the necessary tools before starting your grill! This includes extra wrenches, screwdrivers, and extra propane tanks if needed.

Grilling for the First Time

If you're new to grilling, then you can make it easier by starting off on the right foot.

Start off by preheating your gas grill to 500 °F (260 °C) before adding any food. Once the grill has reached this temperature, add some oil to the grates of the grill and then place your food on it. Be sure that your food covers at least two-thirds of the grate and that you have enough room for some air underneath it as well.

Once the food is placed on your grill and is fully cooked, don't forget to let some of your meat juices drip into a container so that they don't get on the grease tray below.

Should You Salt the Meat before Grilling?

Salt will help to draw the juice from your meat as it cooks, which doesn't allow for as much moisture loss as it would if you didn't have salt on the food. However, there is a limit to how much you should put on your meat. Putting too much salt on your food can be quite a problem because the excess salt will probably draw all of the moisture from your food! If you do decide to add salt to your grilling, be sure that you don't put too much. A good rule of thumb is to use about one teaspoon of salt for every pound of meat that you grill.

Prepare Marinades and Their Exposure Times

Marinades aren't only useful for adding flavor to your food, but they can also be a great way to make sure that your meat doesn't dry out as you grill.

Use marinades that have an acid content of at least 1%. Acids help to break down the fibers in the meat, making it easier for those fibers to soak up the moisture from the marinade. This helps to prevent overcooking and drying out while grilling.

How Long Is Meat after Grilling?

If you don't want to spend all day grilling, then you can open up the grill and use the spatula to transfer your food to a pan or plate as it finishes cooking. If you want to give your food more time on the grill, then you can keep it longer by turning off the heat and letting it rest on the lower level of your grill for 90 minutes. Doing this will let your meat cool down and will leave some of that great barbecue flavor in your meat!

Rubs? Read Many Times, But What Is It?

A rub is a flavorful mixture of spices and herbs that you can add to your grilled food. It can be made from anything from salt, pepper, and garlic powder to cayenne, nutmeg, and cinnamon! It often contains sugar, some type of fat (such as mayonnaise), and some acidic ingredients.

A rub can add great flavors to your food without adding too much extra fat or salt. It will help the smoke flavor penetrate into your meat and give it some great barbecue goodness!

The 6 Basic Rules of Grill

Don't be scared of your grill. You're not cooking on the sidewalk!

Don't Forget to Flip Your Burgers!

Make sure that you clean your grill before putting it away. If it is too dirty, then the temperature of the grill will change when you re-open it, causing food to burn or smoke while resting or cooking on it.

Keep an Eye on Your Meat!

Make small cuts into your food. This will allow you to see when the inside of your food is done cooking, making it easy for you to know when to flip your burgers.

Let the grease drip off of your meat so that it doesn't flare up and burn.

CHAPTER 2. USEFUL ACCESSORIES

Whenever new trends emerge, countless manufacturers want to jump on the racing train together with retailers. Grilling is not a completely new thing and the gas grill is not a recent invention either. Nevertheless, the grill was rather a shadowy existence for many years. Things have been looking different for a few years now: no hardware store or garden center can do without an extensive barbecue department. From a small compact grill for a weekend trip to the countryside to a complete garden kitchen, there is really something for everyone here. There is also a huge selection of accessories. It is worth taking a closer look at what is on offer.

Grill Cover

Many gas grills (especially branded appliances) come with a grill cover included. But they can also be purchased separately in universal sizes. The grill covers are made from a hard-wearing film or waterproof fabric. A grill cover protects the grill in the basement or in the storage room from dust and dirt. During the barbecue season, it is primarily to protect it from rain if the barbecue is left in the garden or on the terrace. You just have to make sure that the grill has really cooled down completely before covering it. A cover that has melted onto the hot gas grill can, in the worst case, result in a total loss.

Grill cover—A must-have.

Plancha

The plancha is a kind of pan for the grill. In this context, one often hears or reads "Crickets like the Spaniards." Since meat juices cannot drip into the grill here, you can work with significantly more sauce on the plancha. It also makes it possible to sear meat, sausage, etc., in larger quantities of fat where it is necessary. In the recipe section below, the plancha is included as a useful accessory. However, it is important to choose a model that is suitable for gas barbecues, as the plancha was originally designed for the charcoal grill or the open fire.

Plancha—Once you've used it, you won't want to go without it.

Dutch Oven

Its name sounds like a Dutch oven, but the Dutch oven actually comes from North America. There it was probably used for the first time by Dutch or German immigrants and it spread quickly. It is a cast-iron pot with a well-closing lid. Since the cast iron walls get evenly hot everywhere, the Dutch oven is suitable for frying, cooking, baking, or steaming. The appropriate accessories (lid lifter, storage grid) must be included here. It is now also available as a variant for the gas grill. In the following part of the recipe, it only plays a subordinate role.

Dutch oven—A great thing for die-hard barbecue fans, but not an absolute must-have.

Incense Box

The smoking box is a metal box with a lid and is perforated all around. This is filled with the desired smoking chips and placed on the grill grate. Due to the heat development, it only takes a few moments for the aromatic smoke to unfold. The smoke that arises on the open gas grill cannot penetrate the grilled food next to it as it would with a closed smoker. But this subtle flavoring has a lot to offer and is great if you have no experience with smoking only for those who are curious about food with a smoke flavor.

Incense box—It is an exciting accessory for everyone who wants to vary and try something out when grilling.

Lava Stones

Fans of the charcoal grill may turn up their noses a bit, but the fact is: Lava stones are the link between charcoal and gas grills. Lava stones are placed over the burner or burners and heated by them. This creates an even heat that is reminiscent of the principle with charcoal. Even the typical charcoal aroma develops here at least approximately: When meat juices drip onto the hot lava stones, the usual charcoal vapors develop. These fumes rise and flavor the food to be grilled. It is nice that the lava stones do not wear out. Nevertheless, they should be replaced after a while. Because meat juices and other grilled liquids can hardly be washed out of the lava stones. Since this principle works so well with the lava stones, some gas grills are even offered as "lava stone grills." Then the lava stones are included in the scope of delivery.

Lava stones—A great thing that even convinces skeptics. And mostly also absolutely affordable.

Gas Level Indicator

The gas bottles do not have a level indicator, so this must be connected to the hose if necessary. You can then read on the display how full a gas bottle is. Experience has shown that hardly anyone looks at the level indicator while grilling. The information shown there would also hardly change your grilling behavior. It is more likely to prepare accordingly and ensure that there is sufficient gas supply before grilling. It is then grilled until the gas in the used bottle runs out. Then you can connect a new, full gas bottle if necessary.

Gas level indicator—It is not absolutely necessary if you have provided a sufficiently large gas supply in advance.

BBQ Cutlery

In addition to the obligatory grill tongs, the grill cutlery also includes a sharp, large meat knife, a meat fork, and a spatula. In general, this accessory is highly recommended so that you don't have to improvise with ordinary cutlery or other aids. Speaking of cutlery, sometimes you will find nice suitcases with barbecue cutlery, in which you can also find special cutlery. This is often more robust than the cutlery you normally use, and the knives are sharper.

BBQ cutlery—A useful thing that actually belongs to every grill. It's great that you usually get the grill cutlery in sturdy aluminum cases. Organizing things is fun too.

BBQ Apron

In general, you can also use an ordinary kitchen apron here. A grill apron is stylish because it is often printed with suitable motifs.

BBQ apron—A nice gimmick for the enthusiastic grill. But not necessarily a must-have.

BBQ Gloves

In contrast to a stovetop or oven, a grill gets hot over a large area. Even at the edges, you can often not touch it with bare fingers without the risk of burns. That's why grill gloves are a sensible thing. You can find them in stores either made of thick, sturdy leather, or flexible, modern materials. Then the grill gloves can even be worn for a longer time without the hands getting heat collapsed. In addition, your hands stay clean.

BBQ gloves—Absolutely recommended, of course not only for the gas grill. But please do not buy the first grill gloves you come across, because there are significant differences in design and quality.

Pizza Stone

Should you really cook a pizza on the grill? This question can be argued about. If you answer it with a resounding yes, you definitely need a pizza stone. Its material ensures a uniform temperature under the pizza base and thus a nicely crispy dough.

Pizza stone for the gas grill—A must-have for pizza fans, superfluous for all other grills.

Grill Mat

A grill mat is comparable to a reusable baking paper. It consists of a rubber-like high-tech material that is extremely heat-resistant and extremely flexible at the same time. The advantages are clearly recognizable: the food does not burn on the grill grate, nothing can drip down and the grill remains largely clean. Some of the recipes named here require a grill mat.

Grill mat—A good idea for everyone who does not like the fumes caused by dripping meat juices and would like to have a clean grill. Purists consider so much hygiene on the grill to be play-spoiling bells and whistles.

Grill Brush

A grill brush is an indispensable accessory if you want to take care of your grill and keep it clean so that you can enjoy it for a long time. Usually, it is a combination of a wire brush and a brush with coarse bristles made of a different material. The material and nature of the wire brush ensure that the grill is not damaged when cleaning. This is why it is not advisable to use a conventional wire brush.

Grill brush—An important tool to keep the grill in the best possible condition for a long time. However, it is worthwhile to take a closer look at the grill brushes on offer and to compare their size and properties with your own needs.

Grill Grate Cleaner

Grill grate cleaner is a liquid product that is usually presented in a spray bottle. This agent can dissolve encrusted fats so that the grill is nice and clean again. However, the grill grate cleaner is quite expensive.

Grill grate cleaner—Works well and certainly makes sense. Usually, a grease-dissolving detergent or oven foam will do the job. Both are available for significantly less money.

Grill Thermometer

A grill thermometer is very much appreciated by many gourmets who want to reach a certain temperature for certain grilled food. Then a core temperature sensor for the meat or other grilled food would be an even better purchase. Purists turn up their noses in both cases and pride themselves on not needing such tools.

Grill thermometer—It is not a must-have. But if you don't want to leave anything to chance, you won't go wrong with it.

Meat Thermometer

In numerous meat dishes, the core temperature is very important. This can be determined particularly well with a meat thermometer, also known as a core temperature probe. There are now even wireless versions that connect directly to an app on the smartphone. It's that easy.

Meat thermometer—One should have.

Rotisserie

Many gas grills are already equipped with a rotisserie, on which you can grill a chicken, for example. But there are also special rotisseries as accessories that can be placed on the grill or attached there. Because of this diversity, it is not advisable to just buy any rotisserie spit. So you should inform yourself exactly about the offer and your own possibilities. An advisor at the dealer will also be happy to help. Beware of cheap offers from the Internet: These often come from dubious sources and are in many cases very insecure. The following recipes also include some that require a rotisserie.

Rotisserie—A great thing for the preparation of delicious dishes. But please do not save at the wrong end, because that ultimately comes at the expense of safety and enjoyment.

The Grill Basket

As the name suggests, this is a basket that is mostly made of stainless steel. This basket is also available in a foldable form for grilled fish: the fish is placed between two surfaces, then both of them are folded together and fixed together with an attached clamp. This grill basket can then be easily turned using a long-handled handle. For small vegetables, it often has a taller shape, but a more closely meshed frame. It is somewhat reminiscent of the basket in a deep fryer. A grill basket is a useful accessory for some of the recipes mentioned here.

Grill basket—Definitely interesting for fish and vegetable fans, possibly also for friends of the small Nuremberg sausages.

CHAPTER 3. TIPS AND TRICKS IN DEALING WITH THE GAS GRILL

In principle, you always make a good choice with a gas grill. A gas grill is safe, efficient, and economical; it heats up quickly, does not smoke, does not stink, and can be used where a charcoal grill is not allowed. In addition, the bottom line is that it conserves resources, while tropical wood from questionable sources is repeatedly used for the charcoal sold here.

In general, a gas grill is easy to use and largely self-explanatory. Nevertheless, you should absolutely observe the information provided by the provider or manufacturer and only ever use the grill under the information given there. In addition, the following tips are intended to help make grilling a safe, beautiful, and delicious pleasure.

Choosing the Right Gas Grill

Since grilling with gas is all the rage, you can always find offers for the different types of grills. It becomes clear that gas grills are on the rise. In hardware stores and garden centers, in specialty stores, and sometimes even at the discounter, you can find offers for gas grills from small to large and from simple to technically complex. Countless online retailers also lure you with real or supposed bargains.

So How Do You Find the Right Gas Grill?

First, it depends on the budget available to determine in which price range you can look around. The cheapest gas grills are compact devices that you can take with you to camping. However, these usually only have a single burner, which means that grilling can be less professional. In addition, they are operated with a comparatively unsafe gas cartridge that can no longer be refilled after use. This extra garbage can be avoided with a standard gas grill. Usually, this is a grill cart, the actual grill of which has a lid and several characteristic controls on the front (reminiscent of the knobs on a kitchen stove). These gas grills are already available in stores for a low three-digit amount.

Important: In addition to numerous established retailers, there are also dubious providers online who offer great-looking gas grills at extremely low prices. Apart from the fact that, in many cases, the goods paid for simply do not arrive (i.e., you have fallen for a fake offer), no reliable statement can be made about the security of these devices.

Trustworthy grills can be recognized by the well-known test certificates TÜV GS.

Experience has shown that in established retailers, one can most likely rely on the fact that the devices are tested and safe. This even applies to gas grills, which are offered as a special offer at discount stores.

Other aspects for the right gas grill relate, of course, to the local conditions at home (how much space is available, what is the surface like?) And to requirements: how often should you grill for how many people?

A multi-burner grill is always recommended, and many of the following recipes will also use them. Further information will follow under 2.

What Is the Difference between Direct and Indirect Grilling?

From direct grilling is when the grill food is placed directly over the heat source on the rack. With a charcoal grill with glowing, completely spread out charcoal, direct grilling refers to the entire grate. It is similar to an electric grill if only the entire area can be brought up to temperature, i.e., there are no parts that can be switched off. The gas grill is ideal here, as only very small grills can be heated completely evenly by a single burner. Larger gas grills have several burners that can be turned on and off individually. This always creates areas with reduced heat, in which indirect grilling is possible. Many of the following recipes take advantage of this opportunity. A classic example is the steak, which can be cooked slowly through indirect grilling but can develop a nice crust in zones with direct heat.

Can You Build a Gas Grill Yourself?

With charcoal grills, there seems to be a trend towards do-it-yourself. More and more grills are no longer bought completely ready-made, but assembled from individual components. The advantage seems to be obvious: self-builders can always better consider their own taste, their own needs, and the local possibilities than is possible for grill providers. However, many construction and garden centers have also adapted to this change and offer garden fireplaces with a grill function as a complete kit.

You don't really have to do long research to find the components of a gas grill online. However, it is noticeable that you have to look for the same in the established retail trade. The reason for this is quickly stated: gas is not to be trifled with! It is a very safe matter, provided the devices have been professionally constructed and are always used correctly. However, assembly is always a matter for professionals, because here it really comes down to the little things.

Even if you could theoretically design and build a gas grill yourself, the following applies: hands off! The selection of safe gas grills designed by experienced manufacturers is so large that everyone can find them. The only exception: if you have your own ideas and the necessary capital, you can design your grill together with a recognized specialist company and have it built there. However, you can quickly reach four or even five-digit amounts.

Do You Need Charcoal for the Gas Grill?

What sounds paradoxical at first actually makes sense: When buying, you can opt for a gas grill or a charcoal grill. But there are also hybrid grills that cleverly combine the two. These gas grills offer the option of using a special charcoal insert, i.e., using it as an alternative to gas firing. This is particularly advantageous for all those who cannot or do not want to choose one or the other system when purchasing. In some cases, a charcoal grill can be the best alternative, and the smell and the rising smoke or the rising vapors create a special grill atmosphere. Last but not least, the coal also represents a certain reserve if you want to fire up the grill spontaneously at the weekend but you may not have sufficient gas supplies at home, so you don't have to go out again.

However, it is important to pay attention to the individual information provided by the grill manufacturer. Some of these charcoal inserts require special types of charcoal. Nevertheless, it is (almost) always charcoal, which you can easily get in the supermarket.

If you want a gas grill with a charcoal insert, you should definitely consider this option when buying the gas grill because only a few manufacturers offer such an application. Please never try to modify an actually unsuitable charcoal insert for the gas grill yourself! This can be dangerous in use and release the manufacturer from guarantee and warranty obligations.

How Do You Clean and Maintain a Gas Grill?

Order is half of life. This also applies to the gas grill, especially since it is generally used outdoors. Here it is not only exposed to the usual soiling that occurs when preparing food (especially splashes of fat and sauce). The humidity and fluctuating temperatures are also noticeable on the grill. That is why it is extremely important to clean it thoroughly quickly after grilling.

Ideally, this means that when the gas grill has largely cooled down after grilling, but is not yet completely cold, the grill is best cleaned.

Realistically, even disciplined grill masters are more likely to deal with cleaning and caring for their darling the next day. Because especially in summer, barbecues are often used until late in the evening, you sit together in a cozy atmosphere and simply don't feel like cleaning now. This is generally not a problem at all, but the grill should be protected from moisture and additional dirt (e.g. from the flying ash of a campfire) until the next morning. If possible, it is rolled under a protective canopy. If the outside of the grill is not particularly dirty, you can also use the specially provided protective cover.

There Are Several Options for Cleaning

Most gas grills have the option of burning them clean. This function is known from the oven as "pyrolysis." The grill is heated up as much as possible when it is closed. All organic substances in the grill are then literally burned. The resulting ash is then removed with a stainless steel brush and the associated dustpan as soon as the grill has cooled down again. But there are also special ash vacuums with which you can easily reach and clean hidden corners of the gas grill.

Removable parts of the gas grill can then be cleaned with a mild soapy solution. Dishwashing liquid with lemon is even better because the acid it contains dissolves any remaining fat residues perfectly. On the other hand, chemical cleaning agents should only be used if heavy encrustations or soiling cannot be removed with either the brush or the detergent. Then please follow the recommendations of the grill manufacturer, because these agents can attack components of the grill. In addition, residues left on the grill may be harmful to health.

As with the removable parts, you can then proceed with the device itself. In general, the grill should not be wiped too wet, as moisture is known to cause rust and, if it does not dry out completely, can also encourage new soiling in hidden areas.

Depending on the frequency of use, the grill should be dismantled every four weeks, but at least every three months according to the manufacturer's

•

instructions, so that hidden components can also be cleaned properly. Any defects or damage can also be identified more easily.

Helpful Accessories for Cleaning a Gas Grill

- Gloves
- Mild washing-up liquid
- Stainless steel brush
- Brass brush
- Sharp kitchen knife
- Dish sponge
- Fine steel wool, possibly as a cleaning sponge

The outside of the grill can be cleaned in a similar way to the appliances in the kitchen. Here, it is advisable to clean the surfaces with mild detergent. An old tea towel from the kitchen is perfect for drying the device afterward so that rust doesn't stand a chance. Nevertheless, after cleaning, the grill should be left in a protected, dry place for at least an hour before it is packed with a protective cover. Undiscovered moisture residues can still evaporate during this time.

If the gas grill is only used during the warm months, the following steps are advisable:

- In good time before the first barbecue pleasure of the year, take the barbecue outside, remove its protective cover and examine it for possible damage.
- If dust has accumulated in the grill, it is best to disassemble the grill so that all components can be thoroughly cleaned.
- After the last barbecue party in autumn, the grill should be cleaned as thoroughly as possible. If so specified by the manufacturer, some parts are finally greased. Then the grill can overwinter in its protective cover. An optimal winter quarter is a dry, dirt and dust-free environment with moderate temperatures.

MEAT RECIPES
BURGER, STEAKS, LAMB, BEEF, POULTRY, GAME, AND PORK

CHAPTER 4. MEAT RECIPES
BURGER, STEAKS, LAMB, BEEF, POULTRY, GAME, AND PORK

1. Marinated Pork Chops

 10 mins   10 mins

 20 mins   4

- 4 pork chops
- ¼ tsp. cayenne
- ½ tsp. pepper
- 1 tsp. garlic, minced
- 2 tbsp. olive oil
- ¼ cup soy sauce
- ⅓ cup Worcestershire sauce
- ⅓ cup balsamic vinegar
- Salt to taste

1. Add the pork chops and the remaining ingredients into a zip-lock bag. Seal the bag, shake well, and place it in the refrigerator for 4 hours.
2. Preheat the grill to medium heat.
3. Spray the grill top with cooking spray.

4. Place the marinated pork chops on the hot grill top and cook for 3–5 minutes on each side or until the internal temperature reaches 145 °F (60 °C) .
5. Serve and enjoy.

Cal: 351kcal │ Carb: 5.9g │ Fat: 26.9g │ Prot: 19.1g │ Sugar: 4.4g │ Cholesterol: 69mg

2. Easy Sirloin Steaks

 10 mins   15 mins

 25 mins   4

- 4 top sirloin steaks
- 1 tbsp. Montreal steak seasoning
- Salt and pepper to taste

1. Season the steaks with Montreal steak seasoning, pepper, and salt.
2. Preheat the grill to medium heat.
3. Spray the grill top with cooking spray.

4. Place the steaks on the hot grill top and cook for 3—5 minutes on each side or until the internal temperature reaches 145 °F (60 °C) .
5. Serve and enjoy.

 Cal: 163kcal | Carb: 0g | Fat: 5.3g | Prot: 25.8g | Sugar: 0g | Cholesterol: 76mg

3. Quick & Easy Marinated Pork Chops

 10 mins   10 mins

 20 mins   4

- 4 pork chops
- 1 tsp. garlic, minced
- ½ tsp. pepper
- 2 tbsp. Worcestershire sauce
- ¼ cup soy sauce
- ¼ cup olive oil
- ¼ tsp. cayenne
- Salt to taste

1. Add the pork chops and the remaining ingredients into a mixing bowl and mix well. Allow marinating for 2 hours.
2. Preheat the grill to high heat.
3. Spray the grill top with cooking spray.

4. Place the pork chops on the hot grill top and cook for 3—5 minutes on each side or until the internal temperature reaches 145 °F (60 °C) .
5. Serve and enjoy.

 Cal: 382kcal | Carb: 3.2g | Fat: 32.5g | Prot: 19.1g | Sugar: 1.8g | Cholesterol: 69mg

4. Delicious Boneless Pork Chops

 10 mins   12 mins

 22 mins   4

- 4 pork chops, boneless

For Rub:
- ½ tsp. ground ginger
- ½ tsp. ground cumin
- 2 tbsp. brown sugar
- ½ tsp. dry mustard
- 1 tsp. pepper
- 1 tsp. garlic powder
- 1 tbsp. sugar
- 1 ½ tbsp. paprika

1. Add the pork chops and the rub ingredients into a mixing bowl and mix well.
2. Preheat the grill to high heat.
3. Spray the grill top with cooking spray.
4. Place the pork chops on the hot grill top and cook for 6 minutes on each side or until the internal temperature reaches 145 °F (60 °C).
5. Serve and enjoy.

 Cal: 299kcal | Carb: 10.1g | Fat: 20.4g | Prot: 18.7g | Sugar: 7.9g | Cholesterol: 69mg

5. <u>Flavors Balsamic Pork Chops</u>

 10 mins   15 mins

 25 mins   4

- 4 pork chops
- 1 tsp. dried rosemary
- 1/8 tsp. chili flakes
- ½ tsp. pepper
- 1 tsp. garlic, minced
- 2 tbsp. Dijon mustard
- 3 tbsp. olive oil
- ½ cup balsamic vinegar
- ¾ tsp. salt

1. Add the pork chops and the remaining ingredients into a zip-lock bag. Seal the bag, shake well, and place it in the refrigerator for 4 hours.
2. Preheat the grill to medium heat.
3. Spray the grill top with cooking spray.
4. Place the marinated pork chops on the hot grill top and cook for 6–8 minutes on each side or until the internal temperature reaches 145 °F (60 °C).
5. Serve and enjoy.

 Cal: 360kcal | Carb: 1.3g | Fat: 30.8g | Prot: 18.4g | Sugar: 0.2g | Cholesterol: 69mg

6. <u>Herb Pork Chops</u>

 10 mins   10 mins

 20 mins   6

- 6 pork chops

For Brine:
- 2 thyme sprigs
- 2 bay leaves
- 1 tbsp. coriander seeds
- 1 tbsp. juniper berries
- 1 tbsp. peppercorns
- ½ cup demerara sugar
- Salt to taste

- 1 liter water

1. Add 1 liter of water and all brine ingredients into a pot and bring to boil. Remove the pot from heat and let the brine cool completely.
2. Add the pork chops to the brine and let it marinate for 2 hours.
3. Preheat the grill to high heat.
4. Spray the grill top with cooking spray.
5. Place the pork chops on the hot grill top and cook for 4–5 minutes on each side.
6. Serve and enjoy.

Cal: 306kcal | Carb: 12.9g | Fat: 20g | Prot: 18.2g | Sugar: 11.7g | Cholesterol: 69mg

7. Dijon Pork Skewers

 10 mins   12 mins

 22 mins   4

- 1 ½ lb. (230 g) pork loin, cut into 1-inch (2,5 cm) cubes
- 2 cups mushrooms
- 2 cups cherry tomatoes
- 2 cups onion, cut into pieces
- 2 cups bell peppers, cut into pieces

For Marinade:
- ½ cup vinaigrette

- ¼ cup Dijon mustard
- Salt and pepper to taste

1. Add the pork cubes and the marinade ingredients into a mixing bowl and mix well and let it marinate for 30 minutes.
2. Thread the marinated pork cubes, mushrooms, tomatoes, onion, and bell peppers onto the skewers.
3. Preheat the grill to high heat.
4. Place the skewers on the hot grill top and cook for 5–7 minutes on each side or until cooked through.
5. Serve and enjoy.

Cal: 628kcal | Carb: 16.2g | Fat: 40.5g | Prot: 50.3g | Sugar: 9.3g | Cholesterol: 136mg

8. Moist Pork Chops

 10 mins   14 mins

 24 mins   4

- 4 pork chops
- 2 tsp. Montreal marinade
- 2 tbsp. soy sauce
- ¼ cup olive oil

1. Add the pork chops and the remaining ingredients into a bowl and mix well and let it marinate for 6 hours.
2. Preheat the grill to high heat.
3. Spray the grill top with cooking spray.
4. Place the pork chops on the hot grill top and cook for 5–7 minutes on each side.
5. Serve and enjoy.

Cal: 373kcal | Carb: 1.2g | Fat: 32.7g | Prot: 18.6g | Sugar: 0.1g | Cholesterol: 69mg

9. Greek Lamb Patties

 10 mins   10 mins

 20 mins   5

- 1 egg
- 1 lb. (450 g) ground lamb
- ½ tsp. sumac
- 1 ½ tsp. ground coriander
- 2 tsp. harissa paste
- 1 tsp. ground cumin
- ¼ cup parsley, chopped
- 1 tsp. garlic, minced
- 1 small onion, minced
- ½ cup breadcrumbs
- Salt and pepper to taste

1. Add all ingredients into a bowl and mix until well combined.
2. Preheat the grill to high heat.
3. Spray the grill top with cooking spray.
4. Make patties from the mixture and place them on the hot grill top and cook for 5 minutes on each side.
5. Serve and enjoy.

Cal: 233kcal | Carb: 9.7g | Fat: 8.2g | Prot: 28.4g | Sugar: 1.4g | Cholesterol: 114mg

10. Pork Patties

 10 mins   10 mins

 20 mins   8

- 1 lb. (450 g) ground pork
- 1/8 tsp. red pepper, crushed
- ¾ tsp. pepper
- ½ tsp. onion powder
- 1 tsp. garlic powder
- 1/8 tsp. ground nutmeg
- ½ tsp. dried thyme
- ¾ tsp. ground sage
- ¾ tsp. fennel seeds
- ½ tsp. salt

1. Add all ingredients into a bowl and mix until well combined.
2. Preheat the grill to high heat.
3. Spray the grill top with cooking spray.
4. Make patties from the mixture and place them on the hot grill top and cook for 5 minutes on each side.
5. Serve and enjoy.

 Cal: 85kcal | Carb: 0.8g | Fat: 2.1g | Prot: 15g | Sugar: 0.2g | Cholesterol: 41mg

11. Juicy Beef Burger Patties

 10 mins   12 mins

 22 mins   6

- 2 lb. (910 g) ground beef
- 2 tbsp. Worcestershire sauce
- ¾ cup onion, chopped
- ½ tsp. pepper
- ½ tsp. salt

1. Add all ingredients into a bowl and mix until well combined.
2. Preheat the grill to high heat.
3. Spray the grill top with cooking spray.

4. Make patties from the mixture and place them on the hot grill top and cook for 5 minutes on each side.
5. Serve and enjoy.

 Cal: 292kcal | Carb: 2.5g | Fat: 9.4g | Prot: 46.1g | Sugar: 1.6g | Cholesterol: 135mg

12. Pork Pineapple Skewers

 10 mins   10 mins

 20 mins   4

- 1 lb. (450 g) pork fillet, cut into chunks
- 2 cups pineapple cubes
- 1 lime juice
- 1 tbsp. hot sauce
- 1 tsp. ground allspice
- 2 tbsp. Creole seasoning

1. Add pork, pineapple cubes, lime juice, hot sauce, allspice, and seasoning into a bowl and mix well.
2. Preheat the grill to high heat.
3. Spray the grill top with cooking spray.
4. Thread the pork and pineapple pieces onto the skewers.
5. Place the skewers on the hot grill top and cook until pork is cooked.

6. Serve and enjoy.

 Cal: 307kcal | Carb: 11.2g | Fat: 14.5g | Prot: 32g | Sugar: 8.2g | Cholesterol: 85mg

13. **Beef Skewers**

 10 mins   15 mins

 25 mins   4

- 1 lb. (450 g) beef sirloin tips
- 1 zucchini, cut into chunks

For Marinade:

- ¼ cup olive oil
- 1 jalapeno pepper
- ½ tbsp. lime juice
- 1 ½ tbsp. red wine vinegar
- 1 tsp. dried oregano
- 2 garlic cloves
- 1 cup cilantro

1. Add all marinade ingredients into a blender and blend until smooth.
2. Pour the blended mixture into the mixing bowl. Add beef tips and mix well and let it marinate for 30 minutes.
3. Thread the marinated beef tips and zucchini chunks onto the skewers.

4. Preheat the grill to high heat.
5. Spray the grill top with cooking spray.
6. Place the skewers on the hot grill top and cook for 7–8 minutes or until beef tips are cooked.
7. Serve and enjoy.

 Cal: 179kcal | Carb: 3.3g | Fat: 14.3g | Prot: 11.4g | Sugar: 1.2g | Cholesterol: 0mg

1. Serve and enjoy.

 Cal: 251kcal | Carb: 1g | Fat: 16.3g | Prot: 22.6g | Sugar: 0.2g | Cholesterol: 121mg

14. **Pineapple Beef Burger Patties**

 10 mins   8 mins

 18 mins   4

- 1 ¼ lb. (110 g) ground beef
- 2 pineapple slices, chopped
- ¼ tsp. pepper
- 1 garlic clove, minced
- 1 tsp. ginger, grated
- ¼ cup green onions, chopped
- ¼ cup soy sauce
- Salt to taste

1. Add all ingredients into a bowl and mix until well combined.
2. Preheat the grill to high heat.
3. Spray the grill top with cooking spray.
4. Make patties from the mixture and place them on the hot grill top and cook for 4 minutes on each side.
5. Serve and enjoy.

 Cal: 135kcal │ Carb: 13.1g │ Fat: 5.3g │ Prot: 9.8g │ Sugar: 8.6g │ Cholesterol: 28mg

15. Steak Sandwich

10 mins   10 mins

20 mins   2

- ¼ lb. (110 g) steaks, cooked and sliced
- 2 tbsp. chimichurri sauce
- 1 tbsp. butter
- 4 bread slices
- 4 cheese slices

1. Spread butter on one side of each bread slice.

2. Take 2 bread slices and spread with chimichurri sauce and top with steak and cheese.
3. Cover with the remaining bread slices.
4. Preheat the grill to high heat.
5. Spray the grill top with cooking spray.
6. Place the sandwich on the hot grill top and cook for 5 minutes or until golden brown from both sides.
7. Serve and enjoy.

 Cal: 617kcal │ Carb: 11.8g │ Fat: 46.8g │ Prot: 36.4g │ Sugar: 1.6g │ Cholesterol: 125mg

16. Tomato Roast Beef Sandwich

10 mins   10 mins

20 mins   2

- 4 bread slices
- ½ lb. (230 g) deli roast beef slices
- 2 tbsp. mayonnaise
- 1 tbsp. butter
- ½ onion, sliced
- 1 tomato, sliced
- 4 cheese slices

1. Spread butter on one side of each bread slice.
2. Take 4 bread slices and spread with mayo and top with beef, cheese, tomatoes, and onion.
3. Cover with the remaining bread slices.
4. Preheat the grill to high heat.
5. Spray the grill top with cooking spray.
6. Place the sandwich on the hot grill top and cook for 5 minutes or until golden brown from both sides.
7. Serve and enjoy.

Cal: 617kcal | Carb: 17.1g | Fat: 35.9g | Prot: 53.9g | Sugar: 4g | Cholesterol: 177mg

17. Dijon Beef Burger Patties

 10 mins   10 mins

 20 mins   4

- 1 lb. (450 g) ground beef
- ½ tsp. pepper
- ¾ tbsp. Worcestershire sauce
- 1 tbsp. Dijon mustard
- 1/8 tsp. cayenne
- 1/8 tsp. chili flakes
- 1 tbsp. parsley, chopped
- ½ tsp. salt

1. Add all ingredients into a bowl and mix until well combined.
2. Preheat the grill to high heat.
3. Spray the grill top with cooking spray.
4. Make patties from the mixture and place them on the hot grill top and cook for 5 minutes on each side.
5. Serve and enjoy.

Cal: 217kcal | Carb: 1g | Fat: 7.3g | Prot: 34.6g | Sugar: 0.6g | Cholesterol: 101mg

18. Classic Burger Patties

 10 mins   12 mins

 22 mins   4

- 1 lb. (450 g) ground beef
- ½ tsp. paprika
- ½ tsp. dried dill
- ½ tsp. onion powder
- ½ tsp. garlic powder
- 2 tsp. dried parsley
- 1/8 tsp. cayenne
- Salt and pepper to taste

1. Add all ingredients into a bowl and mix until well combined.
2. Preheat the grill to high heat.
3. Spray the grill top with cooking spray.
4. Make patties from the mixture and place them on the hot grill top and cook for 4–6 minutes on each side.
5. Serve and enjoy.

 Cal: 215kcal | Carb: 0.7g | Fat: 7.1g | Prot: 34.6g | Sugar: 0.2g | Cholesterol: 101mg

19. Lemon Rosemary Cornish Hen

 10 mins   30 mins

 40 mins   2

- 1 Cornish hen, spatchcocked
- 1 lemon juice
- 1 tsp. rosemary, chopped
- 2 tbsp. soy sauce

1. In a small bowl, mix lemon juice, rosemary, and soy sauce.

2. Preheat the grill to high heat.
3. Spray the grill top with cooking spray.
4. Brush the Cornish hen with the lemon juice mixture and place it on the hot grill top and cook for 20 minutes.
5. Flip the hen and cook until the internal temperature reaches 160 °F (70 °C).
6. Serve and enjoy.

Cal: 164kcal | Carb: 2.1g | Fat: 4.6g | Prot: 26.9g | Sugar: 0.8g | Cholesterol: 117mg

20. Flavorful Cornish Hen

 10 mins   30 mins

 40 mins   2

- 1 Cornish hen, spatchcocked
- ½ tsp. ground thyme
- ½ tbsp. onion powder
- ½ tbsp. smoked paprika
- ¼ tsp. pepper
- ¼ tsp. sage

1. Mix together thyme, onion powder, paprika, pepper, and sage and rub all over the hen.
2. Preheat the grill to high heat.
3. Spray the grill top with cooking spray.

4. Place the hen on the hot grill top and cook for 20 minutes.
5. Flip the hen and cook until the internal temperature reaches 160 °F (70 °C).
6. Serve and enjoy.

 Cal: 160kcal | Carb: 2.7g | Fat: 4.5g | Prot: 26.1g | Sugar: 0.8g | Cholesterol: 117mg

21. Simple Cornish Hen

 10 mins 30 mins

 40 mins 2

- 1 Cornish hen, spatchcocked
- 1 tbsp. olive oil
- Salt and pepper to taste

1. Brush the hen with oil and season with pepper and salt.
2. Preheat the grill to high heat.
3. Spray the grill top with cooking spray.
4. Place the hen on the hot grill top and cook for 20 minutes.
5. Flip the hen and cook until the internal temperature reaches 160 °F (70 °C).
6. Serve and enjoy.

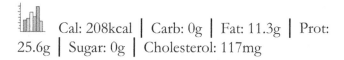 Cal: 208kcal | Carb: 0g | Fat: 11.3g | Prot: 25.6g | Sugar: 0g | Cholesterol: 117mg

22. Classic Cornish Hens

 10 mins 40 mins

 50 mins 4

- 2 Cornish hens, spatchcocked
- 1 tbsp. lemon juice
- 1 tbsp. hot sauce
- ½ cup butter, melted
- Salt and pepper to taste

1. Season the hens with pepper and salt.
2. In a small bowl, mix together lemon juice, hot sauce, and butter.
3. Brush the lemon juice mixture over the hens.
4. Preheat the grill to high heat.
5. Spray the grill top with cooking spray.
6. Place the hens on the hot grill top and cook for 35–40 minutes or until the internal temperature reaches 160 °F (70 °C).
7. Serve and enjoy.

Cal: 352kcal | Carb: 0.2g | Fat: 27.3g | Prot: 25.9g | Sugar: 0.2g | Cholesterol: 178mg

23. Asian Cornish Hens

 10 mins   30 mins

 40 mins   4

- 2 Cornish hens, spatchcocked

For Marinade:

- 1 tbsp. sesame oil
- 2 tbsp. cilantro, chopped
- ¼ cup vegetable oil
- ½ cup soy sauce
- 1 tbsp. ginger, grated
- 3 garlic cloves, minced
- Salt and pepper to taste

1. Add all marinade ingredients into a zip-lock bag and mix well. Add the hens into the bag, seal the bag, and place them in the refrigerator for 6 hours.
2. Preheat the grill to high heat.
3. Spray the grill top with cooking spray.
4. Place the marinated hens on the hot grill top and cook for 30 minutes or until the internal temperature reaches 160 °F (70 °C) .
5. Serve and enjoy.

Cal: 323kcal │ Carb: 4.2g │ Fat: 21.4g │ Prot: 27.9g │ Sugar: 0.6g │ Cholesterol: 117mg

24. Delicious Chicken Fillets

 10 mins   10 mins

 20 mins   4

- 10 chicken fillets

For Marinade:

- 1 bay leaf
- ½ tsp. dried thyme
- ½ tsp. pepper
- ½ tsp. ginger powder
- ½ tsp. turmeric powder
- 1 tbsp. garlic, minced
- 1 lemon zest, grated
- ½ cup olive oil
- ½ cup soy sauce

1. Add all marinade ingredients into a zip-lock bag and mix well. Add chicken fillets into the bag, seal the bag, shake well, and place in the refrigerator for 6 hours.
2. Preheat the grill to high heat.
3. Spray the grill top with cooking spray.
4. Place the marinated chicken fillets on the hot grill top and cook for 5 minutes on each side.
5. Serve and enjoy.

Cal: 937kcal | Carb: 5.2g | Fat: 52.4g | Prot: 108g | Sugar: 0.9g | Cholesterol: 325mg

25. Teriyaki Chicken

 10 mins   15 mins

 25 mins   8

- 2 lb. (910 g) chicken breasts, boneless and cut into 1-inch (2,5 cm) pieces
- 1 tsp. olive oil
- 2 garlic cloves, minced
- 2 tsp. ginger, grated
- 1 tsp. apple cider vinegar
- 1 tbsp. honey
- ¼ cup coconut aminos

1. Add the chicken and the remaining ingredients into a mixing bowl and mix well. Allow marinating for 30 minutes.
2. Thread the marinated chicken onto the skewers.
3. Preheat the grill to medium heat.
4. Spray the grill top with cooking spray.
5. Place the chicken skewers on the hot grill top and cook for 12–15 minutes. Turn the skewers 2–3 times.
6. Serve and enjoy.

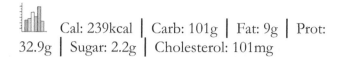 Cal: 239kcal | Carb: 101g | Fat: 9g | Prot: 32.9g | Sugar: 2.2g | Cholesterol: 101mg

26. Turkey Burger Patties

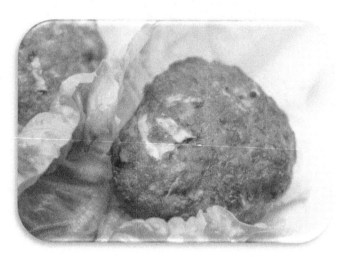

 10 mins   10 mins

 20 mins   4

- 1 lb. (450 g) ground turkey
- 1 tbsp. garlic powder
- 1 ½ tbsp. dried parsley
- 3 oz. (85 g) onion, diced
- Salt and pepper to taste

1. Add all ingredients into a bowl and mix until well combined.
2. Preheat the grill to high heat.
3. Spray the grill top with cooking spray.
4. Make patties from the mixture and place them on the hot grill top and cook for 5 minutes on each side.
5. Serve and enjoy.

Cal: 237kcal | Carb: 3.6g | Fat: 12.5g | Prot: 31.7g | Sugar: 1.4g | Cholesterol: 116mg

27. Ranch Chicken Burger Patties

 10 mins   10 mins

 20 mins   4

- 1 lb. (450 g) ground chicken
- 1 cup cheddar cheese, shredded

⅓ cup bacon, cooked and chopped

1 oz. (28 g) ranch seasoning mix

1. Add all ingredients into a bowl and mix until well combined.
2. Preheat the grill to high heat.
3. Spray the grill top with cooking spray.
4. Make patties from the mixture and place them on the hot grill top and cook for 5 minutes on each side.
5. Serve and enjoy.

Cal: 404kcal | Carb: 0.5g | Fat: 22.2g | Prot: 43.8g | Sugar: 0.2g | Cholesterol: 142mg

28. Moroccan Chicken

 10 mins   10 mins

 20 mins   4

- 4 chicken breasts, boneless and cut into 1-inch (2,5 cm) pieces
- ¼ tsp. turmeric
- ½ tsp. ground cinnamon
- 1 tsp. paprika
- 1 tsp. ground coriander
- 1 ½ tsp. ground cumin
- 1 tbsp. ginger, grated
- 1 tbsp. garlic, minced
- 2 tbsp. lemon juice
- ¼ cup olive oil
- Salt and pepper to taste

1. Add the chicken and the remaining ingredients into a zip-lock bag. Seal the bag, shake well, and place it in the refrigerator overnight.
2. Preheat the grill to high heat.
3. Spray the grill top with cooking spray.
4. Place the marinated chicken on the hot grill top and cook for 4–5 minutes on each side.
5. Serve and enjoy.

Cal: 401kcal | Carb: 2.8g | Fat: 23.8g | Prot: 42.8g | Sugar: 0.3g | Cholesterol: 130mg

29. Juicy & Tender Chicken Breast

 10 mins   10 mins

 20 mins   4

- 4 chicken breasts, boneless and skinless

For Marinade:
- 1 tsp. Dijon mustard
- 1 tsp. lemon zest
- 2 tbsp. lemon juice
- 2 tbsp. honey
- 1 tsp. onion powder
- 2 tsp. garlic powder
- ¼ cup vinegar
- ½ cup olive oil
- ½ tsp. pepper
- ¼ tsp. salt

1. Add the chicken and all the marinade ingredients into a zip-lock bag. Seal the bag, shake well, and place it in the refrigerator overnight.
2. Preheat the grill to high heat.

3. Spray the grill top with cooking spray.
4. Place the marinated chicken on the hot grill top and cook for 4–5 minutes on each side.
5. Serve and enjoy.

 Cal: 539kcal | Carb: 10.8g | Fat: 36.2g | Prot: 42.7g | Sugar: 9.4g | Cholesterol: 130mg

30. Flavorful Italian Chicken

 10 mins   14 mins

 24 mins   4

- 1 ½ lb. (230 g) chicken breasts, boneless and skinless
- 1 tbsp. olive oil
- 2 tbsp. garlic powder
- 2 tbsp. dried basil
- 2 tbsp. dried thyme
- 2 tbsp. dried oregano
- Salt and pepper to taste

1. In a small bowl, mix together oil, garlic powder, basil, thyme, oregano, pepper, and salt.
2. Brush the chicken breasts with the olive oil mixture.
3. Preheat the grill to high heat.

4. Place the chicken on the hot grill top and cook for 5–7 minutes on each side.
5. Serve and enjoy.

Cal: 378kcal | Carb: 5.4g | Fat: 16.5g | Prot: 50.3g | Sugar: 1.1g | Cholesterol: 151mg

31. Easy Blackened Chicken

 10 mins   10 mins

 20 mins   4

- 1 lb. (450 g) chicken breasts, boneless and skinless
- 2 tbsp. blackened seasoning
- 2 tbsp. butter, melted

1. Mix together the melted butter and seasoning and rub over the chicken.
2. Preheat the grill to high heat.
3. Spray the grill top with cooking spray.
4. Place the chicken on the hot grill top and cook for 4–5 minutes on each side.
5. Serve and enjoy.

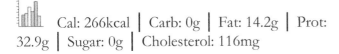 Cal: 266kcal | Carb: 0g | Fat: 14.2g | Prot: 32.9g | Sugar: 0g | Cholesterol: 116mg

32. Perfect Greek Chicken

 10 mins   12 mins

 22 mins   4

- 1 lb. (450 g) chicken breasts, boneless and skinless
- 1 tbsp. red wine vinegar
- 3 tbsp. olive oil
- 3 tbsp. lemon juice
- 1 tbsp. garlic, minced
- ½ tsp. dried thyme
- ½ tsp. dried oregano
- ½ tsp. dried rosemary
- Salt and pepper to taste

1. Add the chicken and the remaining ingredients into a zip-lock bag. Seal the bag, shake well, and place it in the refrigerator overnight.
2. Preheat the grill to high heat.
3. Spray the grill top with cooking spray.
4. Place the marinated chicken on the hot grill top and cook for 5–6 minutes on each side.
5. Serve and enjoy.

Cal: 314kcal | Carb: 1.3g | Fat: 19.1g | Prot: 33.1g | Sugar: 0.3g | Cholesterol: 101mg

33. Marinated Buttermilk Chicken

 10 mins   10 mins

 20 mins   4

- 1 lb. (450 g) chicken breasts, boneless
- 2 tbsp. butter, melted
- 1 tbsp. brown sugar
- ½ tsp. chili powder
- 2 tsp. Italian seasoning
- 1 tsp. onion powder
- 1 tbsp. garlic, minced
- 1 ½ cups buttermilk
- Salt and pepper to taste

1. Add the chicken and the remaining ingredients into a zip-lock bag. Seal the bag, shake well, and place it in the refrigerator overnight.
2. Preheat the grill to high heat.
3. Spray the grill top with cooking spray.
4. Place the marinated chicken on the hot grill top and cook for 4–5 minutes on each side.
5. Serve and enjoy.

Cal: 325kcal │ Carb: 8.2g │ Fat: 15.8g │ Prot: 36.2g │ Sugar: 7g │ Cholesterol: 122mg

34. Tex Mex Chicken

 10 mins   12 mins

 22 mins   4

- 1 lb. (450 g) chicken breasts, boneless
- 2 tbsp. brown sugar
- ½ tsp. pepper
- ¼ tsp. red chili flakes
- ¼ tsp. ground cloves
- ½ tsp. garlic powder
- 1 tsp. dried oregano
- 1 tsp. ground cumin
- 1 tsp. paprika
- 2 tsp. onion powder
- 1 tbsp. chili powder
- 2 tbsp. lime juice
- 1 tbsp. olive oil
- ½ tsp. salt

1. Add the chicken and the remaining ingredients into a zip-lock bag. Seal the bag, shake well, and place in the refrigerator for 1 hour.
2. Preheat the grill to high heat.
3. Spray the grill top with cooking spray.
4. Place the marinated chicken on the hot grill top and cook for 5–6 minutes on each side.

5. Serve and enjoy.

 Cal: 285kcal | Carb: 9.5g | Fat: 12.5g | Prot: 33.6g | Sugar: 5.5g | Cholesterol: 101mg

35.   Tasty Chicken Tenders

 10 mins   8 mins

 18 mins   4

- 1 lb. (450 g) chicken tenders
- ½ tsp. garlic powder
- ½ tsp. paprika
- 2 tsp. thyme
- 1 tbsp. lemon juice
- 3 tbsp. olive oil
- ¼ tsp. pepper
- ½ tsp. salt

1. Add the chicken and the remaining ingredients into a zip-lock bag. Seal the bag, shake well, and place in the refrigerator for 8 hours.
2. Preheat the grill to high heat.
3. Spray the grill top with cooking spray.
4. Place the marinated chicken tenders on the hot grill top and cook for 3–4 minutes on each side.

---

5. Serve and enjoy.

 Cal: 310kcal | Carb: 0.9g | Fat: 19g | Prot: 33g | Sugar: 0.2g | Cholesterol: 101mg

36.   Spicy Chicken Thighs

 10 mins   15 mins

 25 mins   4

- 4 chicken thighs
- ¾ cup olive oil
- 1 tbsp. ground pepper
- ½ small shallot, diced
- 2 garlic cloves, minced
- 2 rosemary sprigs, chopped
- 4 thyme sprigs, chopped
- 1 cup parsley, chopped
- Salt and pepper to taste

1. Add the chicken and the remaining ingredients into a zip-lock bag. Seal the bag, shake well, and place in the refrigerator for 8 hours.
2. Preheat the grill to high heat.
3. Spray the grill top with cooking spray.

4. Place the marinated chicken on the hot grill top and cook for 7–8 minutes on each side.
5. Serve and enjoy.

 Cal: 619kcal | Carb: 3.7g | Fat: 49g | Prot: 43.1g | Sugar: 0.2g | Cholesterol: 130mg

37. Lemon Honey Chicken

 10 mins   15 mins

 25 mins   4

- 1 lb. (450 g) chicken breasts, boneless
- 2 tbsp. honey
- 1 tbsp. Dijon mustard
- 4 lemon juice
- Salt and pepper to taste

1. Add chicken, honey, mustard, lemon juice, pepper, and salt into a mixing bowl and toss well. Allow marinating for 12 hours.
2. Preheat the grill to high heat.
3. Spray the grill top with cooking spray.
4. Place the chicken on the hot grill top and cook for 6–8 minutes on each side.
5. Serve and enjoy.

 Cal: 261kcal | Carb: 9.9g | Fat: 8.9g | Prot: 33.4g | Sugar: 9.6g | Cholesterol: 101mg

38. Chicken with Pesto

 10 mins   10 mins

 20 mins   4

- 4 chicken breasts, boneless and skinless
- ⅓ cup Parmesan cheese, grated
- ⅓ cup olive oil
- 1 tsp. lemon zest
- 2 tbsp. lemon juice
- ¼ cup pine nuts, toasted
- 2 cups baby spinach
- Salt and pepper to taste

1. Season chicken with pepper and salt.
2. Preheat the grill to high heat.
3. Spray the grill top with cooking spray.
4. Place the chicken on the hot grill top and cook for 5 minutes on each side.
5. Add the remaining ingredients except for cheese into a blender and blend until smooth.
6. Mix together the blended mixture and cheese.

7. Pour pesto over the cooked chicken and serve.

 Cal: 537kcal | Carb: 2.5g | Fat: 37g | Prot: 49.1g | Sugar: 0.6g | Cholesterol: 142mg

39. Flavorful Cornish Game Hen

 10 mins   1 h

 1 h and 10 mins   2

- 1 Cornish game hen
- ½ tbsp. olive oil
- ¼ tbsp. poultry seasoning

1. Brush the hen with oil and rub with poultry seasoning.
2. Preheat the grill to high heat.
3. Spray the grill top with cooking spray.
4. Place the hen on the hot grill top and cook from all the sides until brown.
5. Cover the hen with a lid or pan and cook for 60 minutes or until the internal temperature of hen reaches 180 °F (80 °C) .
6. Slice and serve.

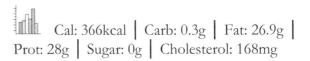 Cal: 366kcal | Carb: 0.3g | Fat: 26.9g | Prot: 28g | Sugar: 0g | Cholesterol: 168mg

40. Flavorful Marinated Cornish Hen

 10 mins   1 h

 1 h and 10 mins   2

- 1 Cornish hen
- 1 cup cold water
- 16 oz. (450 g) apple juice
- 1/8 cup brown sugar
- 1 cinnamon stick
- 1 cup hot water
- ¼ cup salt

1. Add cinnamon, hot water, cold water, apple juice, brown sugar, and salt into a large pot and stir until sugar is dissolved.
2. Add the hen to the brine and place it in the refrigerator for 4 hours.
3. Preheat the grill to high heat.
4. Spray the grill top with cooking spray.
5. Remove the hens from the brine and place them on the hot grill top and cook for 60

minutes or until the internal temperature reaches 160 °F (70 °C) .

6. Slice and serve.

 Cal: 938kcal | Carb: 232g | Fat: 9.5g | Prot: 10g | Sugar: 200g | Cholesterol: 51mg

41. Montreal Seasoned Spatchcocked Hens

 10 mins   1 h

 1 h and 10 mins   2

- 1 Cornish hen
- 1 tbsp. olive oil
- 1 tbsp. Montreal chicken seasoning

1. Cut the backbone of the hens and flatten the breastplate.
2. Brush the hen with oil and rub with Montreal chicken seasoning.
3. Wrap the hens in plastic wrap and place them in the refrigerator for 4 hours.
4. Preheat the grill to high heat.
5. Spray the grill top with cooking spray.
6. Place the marinated hen on the hot grill top and cook for 60 minutes or until the internal temperature reaches 180 °F (80 °C) .
7. Serve and enjoy.

 Cal: 228kcal | Carb: 0g | Fat: 18g | Prot: 14g | Sugar: 0g | Cholesterol: 85mg

42. Rosemary Hen

 10 mins   1 h

 1 h and 10 mins   2

- 1 Cornish game hen
- 1 tbsp. butter, melted
- ½ tbsp. rosemary, minced
- 1 tsp. chicken rub

1. Brush the hens with melted butter.
2. Mix together rosemary and chicken rub.
3. Rub the hen with the rosemary and chicken rub mixture.
4. Preheat the grill to high heat.
5. Spray the grill top with cooking spray.
6. Place the hen on the hot grill top and cook for 60 minutes or until the internal temperature reaches 165 °F (70 °C) .
7. Serve and enjoy.

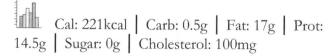 Cal: 221kcal | Carb: 0.5g | Fat: 17g | Prot: 14.5g | Sugar: 0g | Cholesterol: 100mg

43. BBQ Hen

 10 mins   1 h and 30 mins

 1 h and 40 mins   8

- 1 Cornish hen
- 2 tbsp. BBQ rub

1. Preheat the grill to high heat.
2. Spray the grill top with cooking spray.
3. Coat the hens with BBQ rub and place them on the hot grill top and cook for 1 ½ hours or until the internal temperature of the hens reaches 165 °F (70 °C) .
4. Slice and serve.

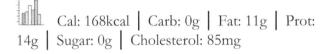 Cal: 168kcal | Carb: 0g | Fat: 11g | Prot: 14g | Sugar: 0g | Cholesterol: 85mg

44. Honey Garlic Cornish Hen

 10 mins   1 h

 1 h and 10 mins   2

- 1 Cornish hen
- 2 garlic cloves, minced
- 1/8 cup honey
- ¼ cup soy sauce
- ¾ cup warm water
- 1 tbsp. cornstarch
- ¼ cup brown sugar
- Salt and pepper to taste

1. Mix together soy sauce, warm water, brown sugar, garlic, cornstarch, and honey.
2. Place the Cornish hen in a baking dish and season with pepper and salt.
3. Pour the marinade over the hen and place it in the refrigerator for 10 hours.
4. Preheat the grill to high heat.
5. Spray the grill top with cooking spray.
6. Place the marinated hen on the hot grill top and cook for 60 minutes or until the internal temperature reaches 165 °F (70 °C) .
7. Serve and enjoy.

Cal: 338kcal | Carb: 42.3g | Fat: 11.8g | Prot: 16.6g | Sugar: 35.6g | Cholesterol: 85mg

45. <u>Sage Thyme Cornish Hen</u>

 10 mins   1 h

 1 h and 10 mins   2

- 1 Cornish hen
- ½ tbsp. paprika
- ¼ tsp. pepper
- ¼ tsp. sage
- ½ tsp. thyme
- ½ tbsp. onion powder

1. In a small bowl, mix together paprika, onion powder, thyme, sage, and pepper.
2. Rub the hen with the paprika mixture.
3. Preheat the grill to high heat.
4. Spray the grill top with cooking spray.
5. Place the hen on the hot grill top and cook for 60 minutes or until the internal temperature reaches 185 °F (90 °C) .
6. Serve and enjoy.

Cal: 180kcal | Carb: 2.7g | Fat: 12g | Prot: 14.9g | Sugar: 0.8g | Cholesterol: 85mg

46. <u>Asian Cornish Hen</u>

 10 mins   1 h

 1 h and 10 mins   2

- 1 Cornish hen
- 1 ½ tsp. Chinese five-spice powder
- 1 ½ tsp. rice wine
- ½ tsp. pepper
- 2 cups water
- 3 tbsp. soy sauce
- 2 tbsp. sugar
- Salt to taste

1. In a large bowl, mix together water, soy sauce, sugar, rice wine, five-spice, pepper, and salt.
2. Place the Cornish hen in the bowl and place it in the refrigerator overnight.
3. Preheat the grill to high heat.
4. Spray the grill top with cooking spray.
5. Remove the Cornish hen from the marinade and place it on the hot grill top and cook for 60 minutes or until the internal temperature reaches 185 °F (90 °C) .
6. Slice and serve.

Cal: 233kcal | Carb: 15.9g | Fat: 11.8g | Prot: 15.9g | Sugar: 13.4g | Cholesterol: 85mg

FISH AND SEAFOOD

CHAPTER 5.
FISH AND SEAFOOD

47. Hibachi Salmon

 Cal: 251kcal | Carb: 3g | Fat: 13g | Prot: 30g

 20 mins   10 mins

 30 mins   4

- 2 lb. (910 g) salmon fillets
- ½ cup teriyaki sauce
- 1 tsp. freshly grated ginger
- 2 garlic cloves
- ¼ cup brown sugar
- 2 tsp. black pepper
- 1 tbsp. maple syrup

1. Mix all the ingredients together in a covered glass bowl or resealable bag, and refrigerate for several hours to overnight.
2. Heat the gas grill to high, and grill the salmon fillets for 3–4 minutes per side until cooked through. The salmon should be homogeneous in color with white juice between the flakes.
3. Let rest for several minutes before serving.

48. Lemon Garlic Shrimp

 20 mins   15 mins

 35 mins   4

- 1 ½ lb. (230 g) shrimp, peeled and deveined
- 1 tbsp. garlic, minced
- ¼ cup butter
- ¼ cup fresh parsley, chopped
- ¼ cup fresh lemon juice
- Salt and pepper to taste

1. Preheat the grill to high heat.
2. Melt butter on the grill top.
3. Add garlic and sauté for 30 seconds.
4. Add the shrimp and season with pepper and salt and cook for 4–5 minutes or until it turns pink.
5. Add lemon juice and parsley and stir well and cook for 2 minutes.
6. Serve and enjoy.

Cal: 312kcal | Carb: 3.9g | Fat: 14.6g |
Prot: 39.2g | Sugar: 0.4g | Cholesterol: 389mg

50. Lemon Garlic Scallops

49. Greek Salmon Fillets

 20 mins   5 mins

 25 mins   2

- 1 lb. (450 g) frozen bay scallops, thawed, rinsed and pat dry
- 1 tsp. garlic, minced
- 2 tbsp. olive oil
- 1 tsp. parsley, chopped
- 1 tsp. lemon juice
- Salt and pepper to taste

1. Preheat the grill to high heat.
2. Add oil to the grill top.
3. Add garlic and sauté for 30 seconds.
4. Add scallops, lemon juice, pepper, and salt, and sauté until the scallops turn opaque.
5. Garnish with parsley and serve.

 Cal: 123kcal | Carb: 0.6g | Fat: 14g | Prot: 0.1g | Sugar: 0.1g | Cholesterol: 0mg

 20 mins   6 mins

 26 mins   2

- 2 salmon fillets
- 1 tbsp. fresh basil, minced
- 1 tbsp. butter, melted
- 1 tbsp. fresh lemon juice
- 1/8 tsp. salt

1. Preheat the grill to high heat.
2. In a small bowl, mix together lemon juice, basil, butter, and salt.
3. Brush the salmon fillets with the lemon mixture and place them on the hot grill top.
4. Cook the salmon for 2–3 minutes. Flip the salmon and cook for 2–3 minutes more.
5. Serve and enjoy.

Cal: 290kcal | Carb: 0.3g | Fat: 16.8g |
Prot: 34.7g | Sugar: 0.2g | Cholesterol: 46mg

51. Salmon Lime Burgers

 Cal: 220kcal | Carb: 6g | Fat: 15g | Prot: 16g

 20 mins   10 mins

 30 mins   2

- 2 hamburger buns, sliced in half
- 1 tbsp. cilantro, fresh minced
- 1/8 tsp. fresh ground pepper
- ½ lb. (230 g) Salmon fillets, skinless, cubed
- ½ tbsp. grated lime zest
- ¼ tsp. sea salt, fine ground
- 1–½ garlic cloves, minced
- ½ tbsp. Dijon mustard
- 1–½ tbsp. shallots, finely chopped
- ½ tbsp. honey
- ½ tbsp. soy sauce

1. Mix all your ingredients in a mixing bowl, except the hamburger buns.
2. Make 2 burger patties that are ½-inch (1,3 cm) thick with this mixture.
3. Preheat your gas grill to medium heat.
4. Once your grill is preheated, place the 2 patties on the grill.
5. Grill your patties for 5 minutes per side. Serve on warm buns and enjoy!

52. Healthy Salmon Patties

 20 mins   10 mins

 30 mins   2

- 6 oz. (170 g) can salmon, drained, remove bones, and pat dry
- 2 tbsp. mayonnaise
- ½ cup almond flour
- ¼ tsp. thyme
- 1 egg, lightly beaten
- 2 tbsp. olive oil
- Salt and pepper to taste

1. Add salmon, thyme, egg, mayonnaise, almond flour, pepper, and salt into a mixing bowl and mix until well combined.
2. Preheat the grill to high heat.
3. Add oil to the grill top.
4. Make small patties from the salmon mixture and place them onto the hot grill top and cook for 5–6 minutes.
5. Turn the patties and cook for 3–4 minutes more.
6. Serve and enjoy.

Cal: 530kcal | Carb: 9.8g | Fat: 41g | Prot: 30.6g | Sugar: 1.1g | Cholesterol: 146mg

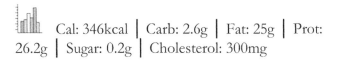 Cal: 346kcal | Carb: 2.6g | Fat: 25g | Prot: 26.2g | Sugar: 0.2g | Cholesterol: 300mg

53. Italian Shrimp

 20 mins   6 mins

 26 mins   4

- 1 lb. (450 g) shrimp, deveined
- 1 tsp. Italian seasoning
- 1 tsp. paprika
- 1 ½ tsp. garlic, minced
- 1 stick butter
- 1 fresh lemon juice
- ¼ tsp. pepper
- ½ tsp. salt

1. Preheat the grill to high heat.
2. Melt butter on the hot grill top.
3. Add garlic and cook for 30 seconds.
4. Toss the shrimp with paprika, Italian seasoning, pepper, and salt.
5. Add the shrimp into the pan and cook for 2–3 minutes per side.
6. Drizzle lemon juice over the shrimp.
7. Stir and serve.

54. Swordfish

 20 mins   15 mins

 35 mins   4

- 4 Swordfish fillets, cut about 1.5 inches (3,8 cm) thick
- 2 tbsp Olive oil
- Sea salt and pepper to taste

1. Preheat the gas grill to high.
2. Drizzle the fillets with olive oil and season with sea salt and black pepper.
3. Place on the grill and cook for 3 minutes per side.
4. Turn the grill down to medium and continue grilling for 5 minutes per side or until the sides of the swordfish are homogeneous in color.
5. Let the fish rest for 5 minutes before serving.

 Cal: 132kcal | Carb: 8g | Fat: 4g | Prot: 22g

55. Honey-Lime Tilapia and Corn Foil Pack

 20 mins 10 mins

 30 mins 4

- 4 fillets tilapia
- 2 tbsp. honey
- 4 limes, thinly sliced
- 2 ears corn, shucked
- 2 tbsp. fresh cilantro leaves
- ¼ cup olive oil
- salt to taste
- Freshly ground black pepper

1. Preheat the grill to high heat.
2. Cut 4 squares of foil about 12" long.
3. Top each piece of foil with a piece of tilapia.
4. Brush the tilapia with honey and top with lime, corn, and cilantro.
5. Drizzle with olive oil and season with sea salt and pepper.
6. Cook until the tilapia is cooked through and the corn is tender, about 15 minutes.

Cal: 319kcal │ Carb: 30.3g │ Fat: 14.7g │ Prot: 24g │ Sodium: 92mg │ Dietary Fiber: 4g

56. Ahi Tuna

 20 mins 6 mins

 26 mins 2

1 Ahi Steaks, cut about 1.5 inches (3,8 cm) thick
2 tbsp Soy sauce
¼ cup Brown sugar
Toasted sesame seeds for topping

1. Preheat the gas grill to the highest setting.
2. Drizzle the soy sauce followed by the brown sugar on both sides of the ahi steaks.
3. Roll the steaks in the sesame seeds.
4. Spray the grill with spray oil.
5. Grill the ahi steaks for 2–3 minutes per side.
6. Let the steaks rest for 5 minutes.
7. Slice thin and serve. Drizzle with more soy sauce if desired.

 Cal: 120kcal │ Carb: 7g │ Fat: 13g │ Prot: 6.8g

57. Gremolata Swordfish Skewers

 20 mins   10 mins

 30 mins   4

1 ½ lb. (230 g) skinless swordfish fillet
2 tsp. lemon zest
3 tbsp. lemon juice
½ cup finely chopped parsley
2 tsp. garlic, minced
¾ tsp. sea salt
¼ tsp. black pepper
2 tbsp. extra-virgin olive oil, plus extra for serving
½ tsp. red pepper flakes
3 lemons, cut into slices

1. Preheat the grill to medium-high heat.
2. Combine lemon zest, parsley, garlic, ¼ teaspoon of salt, and pepper in a small bowl with a fork to make gremolata and set aside.
3. Mix the swordfish pieces with the reserved lemon juice, olive oil, red pepper flakes, and the remaining salt.
4. Thread the swordfish and lemon slices, alternating each, onto the metal skewers.
5. Grill the skewers for 8 to 10 minutes, flipping halfway through or until the fish is cooked through.

6. Place the skewers on a serving platter and sprinkle with gremolata.
7. Drizzle with olive oil and serve.

Cal: 333kcal │ Carb: 1.6g │ Fat: 16g │ Prot: 43.7g │ Sodium: 554mg │ Dietary Fiber: 0.5g

58. Blackened Tilapia

 20 mins   6 mins

 26 mins   4

- 4 tilapia fillets
- 2 tbsp. butter
- 1 tbsp. olive oil

For Seasoning:
- 1 ½ tsp. paprika
- 1 lemon, sliced
- ½ tsp. ground cumin
- 1 tsp. oregano
- ½ tsp. garlic powder
- Salt and pepper to taste

1. In a small bowl, mix together all seasoning ingredients and rub over the fish fillets.
2. Preheat the grill to high heat.
3. Add butter and oil to the hot grill top.

4. Place the fish fillets onto the grill top and cook for 3 minutes.
5. Turn the fish fillets and cook for 3 more minutes or until cooked through.
6. Serve and enjoy.

 Cal: 181kcal | Carb: 1.2g | Fat: 10.5g |
Prot: 21.4g | Sugar: 0.2g | Cholesterol: 70mg

59. Paprika Garlic Shrimp

 20 mins   5 mins

 25 mins   4

- 1 lb. (450 g) shrimp, peeled and cleaned
- 5 garlic cloves, chopped
- 2 tbsp. olive oil
- 1 tbsp. fresh parsley, chopped
- 1 tsp. paprika
- 2 tbsp. butter
- ½ tsp. sea salt

1. Add shrimp, 1 tablespoon of oil, garlic, and salt in a large bowl and toss well and place in the refrigerator for 1 hour.
2. Preheat the grill to high heat.
3. Add the remaining oil and butter to the hot grill top.

4. Once the butter is melted, then add the marinated shrimp and paprika and stir constantly for 2–3 minutes or until the shrimp is cooked.
5. Garnish with parsley and serve.

 Cal: 253kcal | Carb: 3.3g | Fat: 15g | Prot: 26.2g | Sugar: 0.1g | Cholesterol: 254mg

60. Halibut Fillets with Spinach and Olives

 20 mins   10 mins

 30 mins   4

- 4 (6-oz. (170 g)) halibut fillets
- ⅓ cup olive oil
- 4 cups baby spinach
- ¼ cup lemon juice
- 2 oz. (57 g) pitted black olives, halved
- 2 tbsp. flat-leaf parsley, chopped
- 2 tsp. fresh dill, chopped
- Lemon wedges, to serve

1. Preheat the grill to medium heat.

2. Toss the spinach with lemon juice in a mixing bowl and set aside.
3. Brush the fish with olive oil and cook for 3–4 minutes per side, or until cooked through.
4. Remove from heat, cover with foil, and let rest for 5 minutes.
5. Add the remaining oil and cook the spinach for 2 minutes, or until just wilted. Remove from heat.
6. Toss with olives and herbs, then transfer to serving plates with fish, and serve with lemon wedges.

 Cal: 773kcal | Carb: 2.9g | Fat: 36.6g | Prot: 109.3g | Sodium: 1112mg | Dietary Fiber: 1.4g

61. Spicy Grilled Jumbo Shrimp

 20 mins   8 mins

 28 mins   6

- 1–½ lb. (680 g) uncooked jumbo shrimp, peeled and deveined

For the Marinade:
- 2 tbsp. fresh parsley
- 1 bay leaf, dried
- 1 tsp. chili powder
- 1 tsp. garlic powder

- ¼ tsp. cayenne pepper
- ¼ cup olive oil
- ¼ tsp. salt
- 1/8 tsp. pepper

1. Add the marinade ingredients to a food processor and process until smooth.
2. Transfer the marinade to a large mixing bowl.
3. Fold in the shrimp and toss to coat; refrigerate, covered, for 30 minutes.
4. Thread the shrimp onto metal skewers.
5. Preheat the grill to medium heat.
6. Cook for 5–6 minutes, flipping once, until the shrimp turns opaque pink.
7. Serve immediately.

 Cal: 131kcal | Carb: 1g | Fat: 8.5g | Prot: 13.7g | Sodium: 980mg | Dietary Fiber: 0.4g

62. Barbecue Shrimp

 20 mins   5 mins

 25 mins   4

- 3 lb. (1360 g) large raw shrimp, peeled and deveined
- ½ lb. (230 g) butter, melted
- 3 garlic cloves, minced

53

- Zest and juice of 1 lemon
- 2 tsp. sea salt
- 2 tsp. black pepper
- ¼ cup grated Parmesan cheese

1. Place the shrimp on skewers.
2. Mix the remaining ingredients together and set in a bowl.
3. Heat the gas grill to high and grill the shrimp, brushing with the butter mixture, for 2 minutes per side until they are cooked through. They will be solid in color with white and pink tones rather than blue and gray.
4. Serve with grilled summer vegetables, grilled yellow potatoes, or grilled corn (elote).

 Cal: 325kcal | Carb: 8g | Fat: 20g | Prot: 13.7g

63. <u>Salmon Skewers</u>

 20 mins   10 mins

 30 mins   4

- 1 lb. (450 g) salmon fillets, cut into 1-inch (2,5 cm) cubes
- 2 tbsp. soy sauce
- 1 tbsp. toasted sesame seeds
- 1 lime zest
- 2 tsp. olive oil
- 1 ½ tbsp. maple syrup
- 1 tsp. ginger, crushed
- 1 lime juice

1. In a bowl, mix together olive oil, soy sauce, lime zest, lime juice, maple syrup, and ginger.
2. Add the salmon and stir to coat. Set aside for 10 minutes.
3. Preheat the grill to high heat.
4. Slide the marinated salmon pieces onto the skewers and cook on the hot grill top for 8–10 minutes or until cooked through.
5. Sprinkle the salmon skewers with sesame seeds and serve.

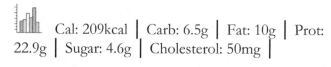 Cal: 209kcal | Carb: 6.5g | Fat: 10g | Prot: 22.9g | Sugar: 4.6g | Cholesterol: 50mg |

VEGETARIAN RECIPES

CHAPTER 6.
VEGETARIAN RECIPES

64. Baked Asparagus Pancetta Cheese Tart

 10 mins 40 mins

 50 mins 5

- 1 sheet puff pastry
- 8 oz. (230 g) asparagus, pencil spears
- 8 oz. (230 g) pancetta, cooked and drained
- 1 cup cream
- 4 eggs
- ¼ cup goat cheese
- 4 tbsp. grated Parmesan cheese
- 1 tbsp. chopped chives
- Black pepper to taste

1. When ready to cook, set the temperature to 375 °F (190 °C) and preheat with the lid closed for 15 minutes.
2. Place the puff pastry on a half sheet tray and score around the perimeter 1-inch (2,5 cm) in from the edges making sure not to cut all the way through. Prick the center of the puff pastry with a fork.
3. Place the sheet tray directly on the grill grate and bake for 15–20 minutes until the pastry has puffed and browned a little bit.
4. While the pastry bakes, combine the cream, 3 eggs, both kinds of cheese, and chives in a small bowl. Whisk to mix well.
5. Remove the sheet tray from the grill and pour the egg mixture into the puff pastry. Lay the asparagus spears on top of the egg mixture and sprinkle with the cooked pancetta.
6. Whisk the remaining egg in a small bowl and brush the top of the pastry with the egg wash.
7. Place back on the grill grate and cook for another 15–20 minutes until the egg mixture is just set.
8. Finish the tart with lemon zest, more chopped chives, and shaved Parmesan.

Cal: 50kcal | Carb: 4g | Fat: 2.5g | Prot: 2g | Fiber: 2g

65. Smoked Mushrooms

 15 mins 45 mins

 1 h 5

- 4 cup Portobello mushrooms, whole and cleaned
- 1 tbsp. canola oil
- 1 tbsp. onion powder
- 1 tbsp. granulated garlic
- 1 tbsp. salt
- 1 tbsp. pepper

1. Put all the ingredients and mix well.
2. Set the grill temperature to 180 °F (80 °C) then place the mushrooms directly on the grill.
3. Smoke the mushrooms for 30 minutes.
4. Increase the temperature to high and cook the mushrooms for a further 15 minutes.
5. Serve and enjoy.

Cal: 1680kcal | Carb: 10g | Fat: 30g | Prot: 4g | Sodium: 514mg | Potassium: 0mg

66. Whole Roasted Cauliflower with Garlic Parmesan Butter

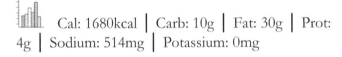

 15 mins   45 mins

 1 h   5

- ¼ cup olive oil
- Salt and pepper to taste
- 1 cauliflower, fresh
- ½ cup butter, melted
- ¼ cup Parmesan cheese, grated
- 2 garlic cloves, minced
- ½ tbsp. parsley, chopped

1. Preheat the gas grill with the lid closed for 15 minutes.
2. Meanwhile, brush the cauliflower with oil then season with salt and pepper.
3. Place the cauliflower in a cast iron and place it on a grill grate.
4. Cook for 45 minutes or until the cauliflower is golden brown and tender
5. Meanwhile, mix butter, cheese, garlic, and parsley in a mixing bowl.
6. In the last 20 minutes of cooking, add the butter mixture.
7. Remove the cauliflower and top with more cheese and parsley if you desire. Enjoy.

Cal: 156kcal | Carb: 8.8g | Fat: 11.1g | Prot: 8.2g | Fiber: 3.7g | Sodium: 316mg | Potassium: 468.2mg

67. Cold Smoked Cheese

5 mins 2 h

 2 h and 5 mins 10

- Ice
- 1 aluminum pan, full-size and disposable
- 1 aluminum pan, half-size and disposable
- Toothpicks
- A block cheese

1. Preheat the grill to 165 °F (70 °C) with the lid closed for 15 minutes.
2. Place a small pan in a large pan. Fill the surrounding of the small pan with ice.
3. Place the cheese in the small pan on top of toothpicks then place the pan on the grill and close the lid.
4. Smoke the cheese for 1 hour, flip the cheese, and smoke for 1 more hour with the lid closed.
5. Remove the cheese from the grill and wrap it in parchment paper. Store in the fridge for 2–3 days for the smoke flavor to mellow. Remove from the fridge and serve. Enjoy.

Cal: 1910kcal | Carb: 2g | Fat: 7g | Prot: 6g | Saturated Fat: 6g | Sugar: 1g | Fiber: 0g | Sodium: 340mg | Potassium: 0mg

68. Grilled Asparagus and Honey Glazed Carrots

 15 mins 35 mins

 50 mins 5

- 1 bunch asparagus, trimmed ends
- 1 lb. (450 g) carrots, peeled
- 2 tbsp. olive oil
- Sea salt to taste
- 2 tbsp. honey
- Lemon zest of 1 lemon

1. Sprinkle the asparagus with oil and sea salt. Drizzle the carrots with honey and salt.
2. Preheat the grill to 165 °F (70 °C) with the lid closed for 15 minutes.
3. Place the carrots in the grill and cook for 15 minutes. Add asparagus and cook for 20 more minutes or until cooked through.
4. Top the carrots and asparagus with lemon zest. Enjoy.

Cal: 1680kcal | Carb: 10g | Fat: 30g | Prot: 4g | Saturated Fat: 2g | Sodium: 514mg

69. Smoked Asparagus

 5 mins   1 h

 1 h and 5 mins   4

- 1 bunch fresh asparagus ends cut
- 2 tbsp. olive oil
- Salt and pepper to taste

1. Preheat your grill to 230 °F (110 °C) .
2. Place the asparagus in a mixing bowl and drizzle with olive oil. Season with salt and pepper.
3. Place the asparagus in a tinfoil sheet and fold the sides so that you create a basket.
4. Smoke the asparagus for 1 hour or until soft turning after half an hour.
5. Remove from the grill and serve. Enjoy.

Cal: 43kcal | Carb: 2g | Fat: 2g | Prot: 3g | Sugar: 2g | Fiber: 2g | Sodium: 148mg

70. Smoked Acorn Squash

 10 mins   2 h

 2 h and 10 mins   6

- 3 tbsp. olive oil
- 3 acorn squash, halved and seeded
- ¼ cup unsalted butter
- ¼ cup brown sugar
- 1 tbsp. cinnamon, ground
- 1 tbsp. chili powder
- 1 tbsp. nutmeg, ground

1. Brush olive oil on the acorn squash cut sides then cover the halves with foil. Poke holes on the foil to allow steam and smoke through.
2. Preheat your grill to 225 °F (110 °C) and smoke the squash for 1 ½–2 hours.
3. Remove the squash from the smoker and allow it to sit.
4. Meanwhile, melt butter, sugar, and spices in a saucepan. Stir well to combine.
5. Remove the foil from the squash and spoon the butter mixture in each squash half. Enjoy.

Cal: 149kcal | Carb: 12g | Fat: 10g | Prot: 2g | Saturated Fat: 5g | Sugar: 0g | Fiber: 2g | Sodium: 19mg | Potassium: 0mg

71. Vegan Smoked Carrot Dogs

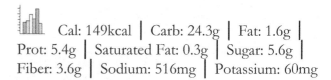 Cal: 149kcal | Carb: 24.3g | Fat: 1.6g | Prot: 5.4g | Saturated Fat: 0.3g | Sugar: 5.6g | Fiber: 3.6g | Sodium: 516mg | Potassium: 60mg

 25 mins   35 mins

 1 h   4

- 4 thick carrots
- 2 tbsp. avocado oil
- 1 tbsp. liquid smoke
- ½ tbsp. garlic powder
- Salt and pepper to taste

1. Preheat the gas grill to 425 °F (220 °C) and line a baking sheet with parchment paper.
2. Peel the carrots and round the edges.
3. In a mixing bowl, mix oil, liquid smoke, garlic, salt, and pepper. Place the carrots on the baking dish then pour the mixture over.
4. Roll the carrots to coat evenly with the mixture and use fingertips to massage the mixture into the carrots.
5. Place in the grill and grill for 35 minutes or until the carrots are fork-tender, ensuring to turn and brush the carrots every 5 minutes with the marinade.
6. Remove from the grill and place the carrots in the hot dog bun. Serve with your favorite toppings and enjoy.

72. Smoked Vegetables

 5 mins   15 mins

 20 mins   6

- 1 ear corn, fresh, husks and silk strands removed
- 1 yellow squash, sliced
- 1 red onion, cut into wedges
- 1 green pepper, cut into strips
- 1 red pepper, cut into strips
- 1 yellow pepper, cut into strips
- 1 cup mushrooms, halved
- 2 tbsp. oil
- 2 tbsp. chicken seasoning

1. Soak the pecan grill in water for an hour. Remove the grill from the water and fill the smoker box with the wet grill.
2. Place the smoker box under the grill and close the lid. Heat the grill on high heat for 10 minutes or until smoke starts coming out from the wood chips.

3. Meanwhile, toss the veggies in oil and seasonings, and then transfer them into a grill basket.
4. Grill for 10 minutes while turning occasionally. Serve and enjoy.

 Cal: 97kcal | Carb: 8g | Fat: 5g | Prot: 2g | Saturated Fat: 2g | Sugar: 1g | Fiber: 3g | Sodium: 251mg | Potassium: 171mg

73. Grill Spicy Sweet Potatoes

 10 mins 35 mins

 45 mins 6

- 2 lb. (910 g) sweet potatoes, cut into chunks
- 1 red onion, chopped
- 2 tbsp. oil
- 2 tbsp. orange{ XE "oranges" } juice
- 1 tbsp. roasted cinnamon
- 1 tbsp. salt
- ¼ tbsp. Chipotle chili pepper

1. Preheat the gas grill to 425 °F (220 °C) with the lid closed.
2. Toss the sweet potatoes with onion, oil, and orange{ XE "oranges" } juice.

3. In a mixing bowl, mix cinnamon, salt, and pepper, then sprinkle the mixture over the sweet potatoes.
4. Spread the potatoes on a lined baking dish in a single layer.
5. Place the baking dish in the grill and grill for 30 minutes or until the sweet potatoes are tender.
6. Serve and enjoy.

 Cal: 145kcal | Carb: 19g | Fat: 5g | Prot: 2g | Saturated Fat: 0g | Sugar: 3g | Fiber: 4g | Sodium: 428mg | Potassium: 230mg

74. Grilled Mexican Street Corn

 5 mins 25 mins

 30 mins 6

- 6 ears corn on the cob
- 1 tbsp. olive oil
- salt and pepper to taste
- ¼ cup mayo
- ¼ cup sour cream
- 1 tbsp. garlic paste
- ½ tbsp. chili powder
- Pinch ground red pepper

- ½ cup coria cheese, crumbled
- ¼ cup cilantro, chopped
- 6 lime wedges

1. Brush the corn with oil.
2. Sprinkle with salt.
3. Place the corn on a gas grill set at 350 °F (180 °C) . Cook for 25 minutes as you turn it occasionally.
4. Meanwhile mix mayo, cream, garlic, chili, and red pepper until well combined.
5. Let the corn rest for some minutes and then brush with the mayo mixture.
6. Sprinkle cottage cheese, more chili powder, and cilantro. Serve with lime wedges. Enjoy.

Cal: 144kcal | Carb: 10g | Fat: 5g | Prot: 0g | Saturated Fat: 2g | Sugar: 0g | Fiber: 0g | Sodium: 136mg | Potassium: 173mg

75. Grilled Stuffed Zucchini

 5 mins   15 mins

 20 mins   8

- 4 zucchini
- 5 tbsp. olive oil
- 2 tbsp. red onion, chopped

- ¼ tbsp. garlic, minced
- ½ cup bread crumbs
- ½ cup mozzarella cheese, shredded
- 1 tbsp. fresh mint
- ½ tbsp. salt
- 3 tbsp. Parmesan cheese

1. Cut the zucchini lengthwise and scoop out the pulp, then brush the shells with oil.
2. In a non-stick skillet, sauté pulp, onion, and the remaining oil. Add garlic and cook for a minute.
3. Add bread crumbs and cook until golden brown. Remove from heat and stir in mozzarella cheese, fresh mint, and salt.
4. Spoon the mixture into the shells and sprinkle Parmesan cheese.
5. Place in a grill and grill for 10 minutes or until the zucchini is tender.

Cal: 186kcal | Carb: 14g | Fat: 10g | Prot: 9g | Saturated Fat: 5g | Sugar: 4g | Fiber: 3g | Sodium: 553mg

76. Bacon-Wrapped Jalapeno Poppers

 10 mins   20 mins

 30 mins   6

- 6 jalapenos, fresh
- 4 oz. (110 g) cream cheese
- ½ cup cheddar cheese, shredded
- 1 tbsp. vegetable rub
- 12 slices cut bacon

1. Preheat the gas grill to 375 °F (190 °C) .
2. Slice the jalapenos lengthwise and scrape the seed and membrane. Rinse them with water and set them aside.
3. In a mixing bowl, mix cream cheese, cheddar cheese, and vegetable rub until well mixed.
4. Fill the jalapeno halves with the mixture and then wrap with the bacon pieces.
5. Smoke for 20 minutes or until the bacon is crispy.
6. Serve and enjoy.

Cal: 1830kcal | Carb: 4g | Fat: 11g | Prot: 6g | Saturated Fat: 6g | Sugar: 4g | Fiber: 1g

77. **Green Beans with Bacon**

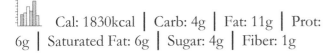

 10 mins   20 mins

 30 mins   6

- 4 strips bacon, chopped

- 1 ½ lb. (230 g) green beans, ends trimmed
- 1 tsp. minced garlic
- 1 tsp. salt
- 4 tbsp. olive oil

1. Switch on the gas grill, fill the grill hopper with flavored grill, power the grill on by using the control panel, select 'smoke' on the temperature dial, or set the temperature to 450 °F (230 °C) and let it preheat for a minimum of 15 minutes.
2. Meanwhile, take a sheet tray, place all the ingredients in it and toss until mixed.
3. When the grill has preheated, open the lid; place the prepared sheet tray on the grill grate, shut the grill, and smoke for 20 minutes until lightly browned and cooked.
4. When done, transfer the green beans to a dish and then serve.

Cal: 93kcal | Carb: 8.2g | Fat: 4.6g | Prot: 5.9g | Fiber: 2.9g

78. **Grilled Potato Salad**

 15 mins   10 mins

 25 mins   8

- 1 ½ lb. (230 g) fingerling potatoes, halved lengthwise
- 1 small jalapeno, sliced
- 10 scallions
- 2 tsp. salt
- 2 tbsp. rice vinegar
- 2 tsp. lemon juice
- ⅔ cup olive oil, divided
- Black pepper to taste

1. Switch on the gas grill, fill the grill hopper with pecan flavored grill, power the grill on by using the control panel, select 'smoke' on the temperature dial, or set the temperature to 450 °F (230 °C) and let it preheat for a minimum of 5 minutes.
2. Meanwhile, prepare the scallions, and for this, brush them with some oil.
3. When the grill has preheated, open the lid, place scallions on the grill grate, shut the grill, and smoke for 3 minutes until lightly charred.
4. Then transfer the scallions to a cutting board, let them cool for 5 minutes, then cut into slices and set aside until required.
5. Brush the potatoes with some oil, season with some salt and black pepper, place the potatoes on the grill grate, and shut the grill for 5 minutes until thoroughly cooked.
6. Then take a large bowl, pour in the remaining oil, add salt, lemon juice, and vinegar and stir until combined.
7. Add grilled scallion and potatoes, toss until well mixed, taste to adjust seasoning, and then serve.

 Cal: 224kcal | Carb: 27g | Fat: 12g | Prot: 1.9g | Fiber: 3.3g

79. **Vegetable Sandwich**

 30 mins   45 mins

 1 h and 15 mins   4

For the Smoked Hummus:
- 1 ½ cups cooked chickpeas
- 1 tbsp. minced garlic
- 1 tsp. salt
- 4 tbsp. lemon juice
- 2 tbsp. olive oil
- ⅓ cup tahini

For the Vegetables:
- 2 large Portobello mushrooms
- 1 small eggplant, destemmed, sliced into strips
- 1 tsp. salt
- 1 small zucchini, trimmed, sliced into strips
- ½ tsp. ground black pepper
- 1 small yellow squash, peeled, sliced into strips
- ¼ cup olive oil

For the Cheese:
- 1 lemon, juiced
- ½ tsp. minced garlic
- ¼ tsp. ground black pepper
- ¼ tsp. salt
- ½ cup ricotta cheese

To Assemble:

- 1 bunch basil, leaves chopped
- 2 heirloom tomatoes, sliced
- 4 ciabatta buns, halved

1. Switch on the gas grill, fill the grill hopper with pecan flavored grill, power the grill on by using the control panel, select 'smoke' on the temperature dial, or set the temperature to 180 °F (80 °C) and let it preheat for a minimum of 15 minutes.
2. Meanwhile, prepare the hummus, and for this, take a sheet tray and spread chickpeas on it.
3. When the grill has preheated, open the lid, place the sheet tray on the grill grate, shut the grill, and smoke for 20 minutes.
4. When done, transfer the chickpeas to a food processor, add the remaining ingredients for the hummus in it, and pulse for 2 minutes until smooth, set aside until required.
5. Change the smoking temperature to 500 °F (260 °C) , shut with lid, and let it preheat for 10 minutes.
6. Meanwhile, prepare vegetables, and for this, take a large bowl, place all the vegetables in it, add salt and black pepper, drizzle with oil and lemon juice, and toss until coated.
7. Place the vegetables on the grill grate, shut with lid, and then smoke the eggplant, zucchini, and squash for 15 minutes and mushrooms for 25 minutes.
8. Meanwhile, prepare the cheese and for this, take a small bowl, place all of the ingredients in it and stir until well combined.
9. Assemble the sandwich for this, cut buns in half lengthwise, spread the prepared hummus on one side, spread cheese on the other side, then stuff with the grilled vegetables and top with tomatoes and basil.
10. Serve straight away.

 Cal: 560kcal | Carb: 45g | Fat: 40g | Prot: 8.3g | Fiber: 6.8g

80. Grilled Sugar Snap Peas

 15 mins　　 10 mins

 25 mins　　 4

- 2 lb. (910 g) sugar snap peas, ends trimmed
- ½ tsp. garlic powder
- 1 tsp. salt
- ⅔ tsp. ground black pepper
- 2 tbsp. olive oil

1. Switch on the gas grill, fill the grill hopper with apple-flavored grill, power the grill on by using the control panel, select 'smoke' on the temperature dial, or set the temperature to 450 °F (230 °C) and let it preheat for a minimum of 15 minutes.
2. Meanwhile, take a medium bowl, place the peas in it, add garlic powder and oil, season with salt and black pepper, toss until mixed, and then spread on the sheet pan.
3. When the grill has preheated, open the lid, place the prepared sheet pan on the grill grate, shut the grill, and smoke for 10 minutes until slightly charred.
4. Serve straight away.

 Cal: 91kcal | Carb: 9g | Fat: 5g | Prot: 4g | Fiber: 3g

81. Cauliflower with Parmesan and Butter

 15 mins   45 mins

 1 h   4

- 1 medium head cauliflower
- 1 tsp. minced garlic
- 1 tsp. salt
- ½ tsp. ground black pepper
- ¼ cup olive oil
- ½ cup melted butter, unsalted
- ½ tbsp. chopped parsley
- ¼ cup shredded Parmesan cheese

1. Switch on the gas grill, fill the grill hopper with flavored grill, power the grill on by using the control panel, select 'smoke' on the temperature dial, or set the temperature to 450 °F (230 °C) and let it preheat for a minimum of 15 minutes.
2. Meanwhile, brush the cauliflower head with oil, season with salt and black pepper, and then place in a skillet pan.
3. When the grill has preheated, open the lid, place the prepared skillet pan on the grill grate, shut the grill, and smoke for 45 minutes until golden brown and the center has turned tender.
4. Meanwhile, take a small bowl, place melted butter in it, and then stir in garlic, parsley, and cheese until combined.
5. Baste the cheese mixture frequently in the last 20 minutes of cooking and, when done, remove the pan from heat and garnish the cauliflower with parsley.
6. Cut it into slices and then serve.

Cal: 128kcal | Carb: 10.8g | Fat: 7.6g | Prot: 7.4g | Fiber: 5g

GRILL BREAD VARIATIONS, TARTE FLAMBÉE, SANDWICH, AND PIZZA

CHAPTER 7.
GRILL BREAD VARIATIONS, TARTE FLAMBÉE, SANDWICH, AND PIZZA

82. Peanut Butter Sandwich

 10 mins 5 mins

 15 mins 1

- 2 bread slices
- ½ banana, cut into slices
- 4 tbsp. peanut butter
- ¼ tsp. cinnamon
- 1 tbsp. honey

1. Take one bread slice and spread it with peanut butter and then top with banana slices.
2. Drizzle with honey and sprinkle with cinnamon. Cover with the remaining bread slice.
3. Preheat the grill to high heat.
4. Spray the grill top with cooking spray.
5. Place the sandwich on the hot grill top and cook for 5 minutes or until golden brown from both sides.

6. Serve and enjoy.

 Cal: 542kcal | Carb: 53g | Fat: 33g | Prot: 18.1g | Sugar: 31.3g | Cholesterol: 0mg

83. Blueberry Sandwich

 10 mins 5 mins

 15 mins 1

- 2 bread slices
- ¼ cup blueberries
- 1 tbsp. cream cheese

1. Take one bread slice and spread it with cream cheese and then top with blueberries. Cover with the remaining bread.
2. Preheat the grill to high heat.
3. Spray grill top with cooking spray.
4. Place sandwich on the hot grill top and cook for 5 minutes or until golden brown from both sides.
5. Servings and enjoy.

68

Cal: 104kcal | Carb: 14.6g | Fat: 4.2g |
Prot: 2.4g | Sugar: 4.4g | Cholesterol: 11mg

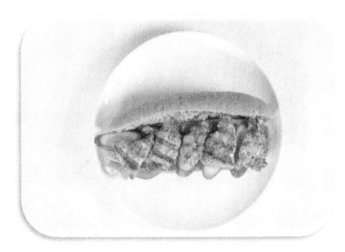 Cal: 732kcal | Carb: 13.1g | Fat: 45.3g |
Prot: 57g | Sugar: 1.9g | Cholesterol: 197mg

84. Chicken Sandwich

 10 mins   5 mins

 15 mins   1

- 2 bread slices
- 1 cup chicken, cooked and chopped
- ½ cup baby spinach
- 1 tbsp. garlic ranch dressing
- 1 tbsp. butter
- 2 tomato slices
- 4 bacon slices, cooked
- 2 cheese slices

1. Spread butter on one side of each bread slice.
2. Take 1 bread slice and spread with garlic ranch dressing and then top with chicken, spinach, bacon, tomato, and cheese.
3. Cover with the remaining bread slice.
4. Preheat the grill to high heat.
5. Spray the grill top with cooking spray.
6. Place the sandwich on the hot grill top and cook for 5 minutes or until golden brown from both sides.
7. Serve and enjoy.

85. Tangy Chicken Sandwiches

 30 mins   15 mins

 45 mins   4

- 2 lb. (910 g) chicken breast, sliced into 4 cutlets
- 2 potato buns, toasted

For the Marinade:
- ½ cup pickle juice
- ½ tbsp. Dijon mustard
- 1 tsp. paprika
- ½ tsp. black pepper
- ½ tsp. salt

1. Mix the marinade ingredients together in a mixing bowl.
2. Place the chicken in the marinade and marinate for 30 minutes in the refrigerator.
3. Preheat the grill to medium-high heat. Wipe off extra marinade and sear the chicken for 7 minutes per side, or until a meat thermometer reaches 165 °F (70 °C) .

4. Allow the chicken to rest for 5 minutes after grilling and serve on toasted buns.

 Cal: 2kcal | Carb: 1.1g | Fat: 6g | Prot: 48.4g | Sodium: 685mg | Dietary Fiber: 0.6g

86. Turkey Pesto Panini

 5 mins   12 mins

 17 mins   2

- ¼ tbsp. olive oil
- 2 slices French bread
- ½ cup pesto sauce
- 3 slices mozzarella cheese
- 2 cups chopped leftover turkey
- 1 Roma tomato, thinly sliced
- 1 avocado, halved, seeded, peeled, and sliced

1. Preheat the grill to medium-high heat.
2. Brush each slice of bread with olive oil on one side.
3. Place 2 slices of bread, olive oil side down, on the grill.
4. Spread 2 tablespoons of pesto over 1 side of the French bread.
5. Top with one slice of mozzarella, turkey, tomatoes, avocado, a second slice of

mozzarella, and top with the second half of bread to make a sandwich; repeat with the remaining slices of bread.
6. Cook until the bread is golden and the cheese is melted, about 2–3 minutes per side.
7. Servings warm with your favorite salad or soup.

 Cal: 1129kcal | Carb: 53.2g | Fat: 70.9g | Prot: 73g | Sodium: 1243mg | Dietary Fiber: 10g

87. Pork Tenderloin Sandwiches

 10 mins   25 mins

 35 mins   6

- 2 (¾-lb.) pork tenderloins
- ½ tsp. garlic powder
- 1 tsp. sea salt
- 1 tsp. dry mustard
- ½ tsp. coarsely ground pepper
- Olive oil, for brushing
- 1 whole-wheat hamburger buns
- ½ tbsp. barbecue sauce

1. Stir the garlic, salt, pepper, and mustard together in a small mixing bowl.

2. Rub the pork tenderloins evenly with olive oil, then the seasoning mix.

3. Preheat the grill to medium-high heat, and cook for 10 to 12 minutes on each side or until a meat thermometer inserted into the thickest portion registers 155 °F (70 °C).

4. Remove from the grill and let stand 10 minutes.

5. Slice thinly, and evenly distribute onto hamburger buns.

6. Drizzle each sandwich with barbecue sauce and serve.

 Cal: 372kcal | Carb: 24.7g | Fat: 13.4g | Prot: 37.2g | Sodium: 694mg | Dietary Fiber: 2.9g

88.　Cheesy Ham and Pineapple Sandwich

 10 mins　　 20 mins

 30 mins　　 4

- 1 (10-oz. (280 g)) package deli sliced ham
- 2 pineapple rings
- 2 slices Swiss cheese
- 8 slices thick bread
- Butter, softened, for brushing

1. Butter one side of all the slices of bread and heat your grill to medium heat.

2. On top of each piece of bread, stack ¼ of the ham, a pineapple ring, and 1 slice of cheese.

3. Place the sandwiches on the grill and top with another slice of bread.

4. Cook until the bottom bread is golden brown, then flip and cook until the other side of the bread is browned and the cheese is melted.

 Cal: 594kcal | Carb: 4.7g | Fat: 40.3g | Prot: 47.7g | Sodium: 3184mg | Dietary Fiber: 0.3g

89.　Grill Pizza Cheese

 10 mins　　 20 mins

 30 mins　　 4

- 8 slices French bread
- 3 tbsp. butter, softened
- ½ cup pizza sauce
- ¼ cup mozzarella cheese
- ½ cup pepperoni diced
- Garlic powder, for dusting
- Oregano, for dusting

1. Spread butter on one side of each French bread slice.

71

2. Place each bread slice butter side down on a piece of aluminum foil and dust with garlic powder and oregano.
3. Spread the pizza sauce on the opposite side of all French bread slices.
4. Top 4 slices of bread with mozzarella cheese, a few slices of pepperoni, and additional mozzarella.
5. Place the remaining French bread slices on top of pizza topped bread, butter side up, to create 4 sandwiches.
6. Preheat the grill to medium heat and place one slice of bread, buttered side down into the grill.
7. Cook for 3 minutes and flip to cook for 3 minutes on the other side; cook until the bread is golden and the cheese is melted.
8. Serve warm and enjoy!

Cal: 305kcal | Carb: 40.4g | Fat: 12g | Prot: 9.4g | Sodium: 664mg | Dietary Fiber: 2.3g

90. **Veggie Pesto Flatbread**

 40 mins   10 mins

 50 mins   4

- 2 flatbreads
- 1 jar pesto
- 1 cup shredded mozzarella cheese

For the Topping:
- ½ cup cherry tomatoes, halved
- 1 small red onion, sliced thin
- 1 red bell pepper, sliced
- 1 yellow bell pepper, sliced
- ½ cup mixed black and green olives, halved
- 1 small yellow squash or zucchini, sliced
- ½ tsp. olive oil
- ¼ tsp. sea salt
- ¼ tsp. black pepper

1. Preheat the grill to low heat.
2. Spread an even amount of pesto onto each flatbread.
3. Top with ½ cup mozzarella cheese each.
4. Mix all the topping ingredients together in a large mixing bowl with a rubber spatula.
5. Lay flatbreads on the grill, and top with an even amount of topping mixture; spreading to the edges of each.
6. Tent the flatbreads with foil for 5 minutes each, or until cheese is just melted.
7. Place flatbreads on a flat surface or cutting board and cut each with a pizza cutter or kitchen scissors.
8. Serve warm!

Cal: 177kcal | Carb: 12.6g | Fat: 11.9g | Prot: 5.5g | Sodium: 482mg | Dietary Fiber: 1.7g

91. Grill Vegetable Pizza

 30 mins   10 mins

 40 mins   6

- 8 small fresh mushrooms, halved
- 1 small zucchini, cut into ¼-inch (0,6 cm) slices
- 1 small yellow pepper, sliced
- 1 small red pepper, sliced
- 1 small red onion, sliced
- 1 tbsp. white wine vinegar
- 1 tbsp. water
- ½ tsp. olive oil, divided
- ½ tsp. dried basil
- ¼ tsp. sea salt
- ¼ tsp. pepper
- 1 prebaked, 12-inch (30,5 cm) thin whole wheat pizza crust
- 1 can (8-oz. (230 g)) pizza sauce
- 2 small tomatoes, chopped
- ½ cups shredded part-skim mozzarella cheese

1. Preheat your grill to medium-high heat.
2. Combine mushrooms, zucchini, peppers, onion, vinegar, water, 3 teaspoons of oil, and seasonings in a large mixing bowl.

3. Transfer to the grill and cook over medium heat for 10 minutes or until tender, stirring often.
4. Brush the crust with the remaining oil and spread with pizza sauce.
5. Top evenly with the grilled vegetables, tomatoes, and cheese.
6. Tent with aluminum foil and grill over medium heat for 5 to 7 minutes or until edges are lightly browned and cheese is melted.
7. Serve warm!

Cal: 111kcal │ Carb: 12.2g │ Fat: 5.4g │ Prot: 5g │ Sodium: 257mg │ Dietary Fiber: 1.7g

92. Bacon Jalapeno Wraps

 5 mins   15 mins

 20 mins   4

- 1 package bacon, uncured and nitrate-free
- 2 fresh jalapeno peppers, halved lengthwise and seeded
- 1 (8-oz. (230 g)) package cream cheese
- 1 dozen toothpicks, soaked

1. Preheat your grill to high heat.
2. Fill jalapeno halves with cream cheese.

3. Wrap each with bacon. Secure with a toothpick.
4. Place on the grill, and cook until the bacon is crispy, about 5 to 7 minutes per side.
5. Remove to a platter to cool and serve warm.

Cal: 379kcal | Carb: 3.5g | Fat: 33.4g | Prot: 16.3g | Sodium: 1453mg | Dietary Fiber: 0.9g

93. Croque Madame

 10 mins   10 mins

 20 mins   2

- ½ tbsp. butter
- ½ tbsp. flour
- ⅔ cup milk
- ¼ slices thick-cut bread
- ⅓ slices black forest ham
- ½ slices gruyere cheese
- Salt and black pepper to taste
- 3 eggs

1. In a small saucepan over medium heat, melt one tablespoon of butter and add the flour. Whisk until just browned and add the milk. Stir until the sauce has thickened. Remove from heat and season with salt and pepper.

2. Heat your grill to medium heat. Butter one side of each slice of bread and add a generous amount of the béchamel sauce to the other side.
3. Place two slices of ham on top of each sandwich and top with the other slice of bread. Place on the grill and cook until golden brown. Flip the sandwiches and top with the gruyere cheese. On the other side of the grill, crack the eggs and cook until the whites are firm.
4. Cook until the other side of the sandwich is golden brown and the gruyere has melted on top. Top each sandwich with a fried egg before serving.

Cal: 538kcal | Carb: 17.8g | Fat: 35.2g | Prot: 36.9g | Sodium: 1019mg | Dietary Fiber: 2.4g

94. Ultimate Grill Cheese

 10 mins   10 mins

 20 mins   4

- 8 slices sourdough bread
- 2 slices provolone cheese
- 2 slices yellow American cheese
- 4 slices sharp cheddar cheese
- 4 slices tomato

74

- 3 tbsp. mayonnaise
- 3 tbsp. butter

1. Heat your grill to medium heat.
2. Butter one side of each piece of bread and spread mayo on the other side.
3. Place the buttered side down on the grill and stack the cheeses on top.
4. Place the other pieces of bread, butter side up, on top of the cheese, and cook until golden brown. Flip and cook until the other piece of bread is golden brown as well and the cheese is melted.
5. Remove from the grill, slice in half, and enjoy.

Cal: 521kcal | Carb: 41.4g | Fat: 30.1g | Prot: 22g | Sodium: 1044mg | Dietary Fiber: 1.7

How to get your free e-book copy

Please send an e-mail to this address

with subject: "free cookbook"

to receive your e-book version:

PeterBeck103@gmail.com

Thank you!

SNACKS &
HANDS DISHES

CHAPTER 8.
SNACKS & HANDS DISHES

95. Tasty Bread Pizza

 Cal: 71kcal | Carb: 11g | Fat: 2.3g | Prot: 2.6g | Sugar: 3.2g | Cholesterol: 2mg

 10 mins   10 mins

 20 mins   4

- 4 bread slices

For Toppings:
- 10 olives, sliced
- 1 small tomato, cubed
- ½ cup bell pepper, cubed
- 1 onion, cubed
- ¼ tsp. red chili flakes
- ½ tsp. oregano
- ½ cup mozzarella cheese, grated
- 2 tbsp. pizza sauce

1. Spread pizza sauce over the bread slices. Top with olives, tomatoes, bell pepper, and onion.
2. Sprinkle with chili flakes, oregano, and cheese.
3. Preheat the grill to medium heat.
4. Place the bread slices on the hot grill top and cover and cook until the cheese is melted.
5. Serve and enjoy.

96. Corn Cakes

 10 mins   10 mins

 20 mins   10

- 4 eggs
- 2 cups corn
- ½ tsp. pepper
- ½ cup cornmeal
- ½ cup flour
- ½ cup cheddar cheese, shredded
- ⅔ cup green onions, sliced
- 1 jalapeno, chopped
- ½ tsp. salt

1. Add the corn into a food processor and process until roughly chopped.
2. Add the corn and the remaining ingredients into a mixing bowl and mix until well combined.

3. Preheat the grill to high heat.
4. Spray the grill top with cooking spray.
5. Make patties from the mixture and place them on the hot grill top and cook until lightly golden brown from both sides.
6. Serve and enjoy.

 Cal: 122kcal | Carb: 16.1g | Fat: 4.3g | Prot: 5.9g | Sugar: 1.4g | Cholesterol: 71mg

97. Tuna Patties

 10 mins   10 mins

 20 mins   4

- 1 egg
- 10 oz. (280 g) can tuna, drained
- 25 crackers, crushed
- ¼ tsp. pepper
- 2 tsp. Dijon mustard
- 1 tbsp. mayonnaise
- ¼ cup onion, chopped
- ¼ tsp. salt

1. Add all ingredients into the bowl and mix until well combined.
2. Preheat the grill to high heat.
3. Spray the grill top with cooking spray.

4. Make patties from the mixture and place them on the hot grill top and cook until lightly golden brown from both sides.
5. Serve and enjoy.

 Cal: 243kcal | Carb: 17.1g | Fat: 9.3g | Prot: 21.5g | Sugar: 1.1g | Cholesterol: 63mg

98. Quick Cheese Toast

 10 mins   8 mins

 18 mins   4

- 8 bread slices
- 4 garlic cloves, minced
- 2 green chilies, chopped
- 1 cup mozzarella cheese, shredded
- 1 cup bell pepper, chopped
- Salt and pepper to taste

1. Mix bell pepper, green chilies, and garlic and spread evenly over the bread slices. Top with cheese, pepper, and salt.
2. Preheat the grill to medium heat.
3. Spray the grill top with cooking spray.
4. Place the bread slices on the hot grill top, cover, and cook until the cheese melts.
5. Serve and enjoy.

Cal: 87kcal | Carb: 13.6g | Fat: 1.9g | Prot: 3.9g | Sugar: 2.8g | Cholesterol: 4mg

 Cal: 124kcal | Carb: 20.4g | Fat: 2.5g | Prot: 5.2g | Sugar: 3.2g | Cholesterol: 55mg

99. Veggie Patties

100. Tomato Avocado Bruschetta

 10 mins   10 mins

 20 mins   6

 10 mins   10 mins

 20 mins   6

- 2 eggs
- 2 tbsp. parsley, chopped
- ½ cup onion, chopped
- 1 cup potatoes, shredded
- 1 cup zucchini, shredded
- 1 cup carrots, shredded
- 1 cup breadcrumbs
- Salt and pepper to taste

- 6 bread slices
- 2 tbsp. olive oil

For Topping:
- 1 tomato, chopped
- 1 garlic clove, minced
- 1 cucumber, diced
- 1 avocado, peeled and diced
- ¼ tsp. sea salt

1. Add all ingredients into a bowl and mix until well combined.
2. Preheat the grill to high heat.
3. Spray the grill top with cooking spray.
4. Make patties from the mixture and place them on the hot grill top and cook until lightly golden brown from both sides.
5. Serve and enjoy.

1. Preheat the grill to high heat.
2. Brush the bread slices with oil and place them on the hot grill top and cook until lightly golden brown from both sides.
3. In a bowl, add all the topping ingredients and mix well.
4. Spoon the topping mixture over the bread slices.
5. Serve and enjoy.

Cal: 142kcal | Carb: 9.8g | Fat: 11.6g |
Prot: 1.8g | Sugar: 1.7g | Cholesterol: 0mg

 Cal: 208kcal | Carb: 18.9g | Fat: 13.3g |
Prot: 3.9g | Sugar: 0.8g | Cholesterol: 0mg

101. **Delicious Guacamole Bruschetta**

 10 mins   10 mins

 20 mins   8

- 8 oz. (230 g) baguette bread, cut into 1-inch (2,5 cm) slices
- 2 tbsp. olive oil

For Topping:
- 2 avocados, diced
- 1 tsp. lemon juice
- 1 tsp. garlic, minced
- Salt and pepper to taste

1. Preheat the grill to high heat.
2. Brush the bread slices with oil and place them on the hot grill top and cook until lightly golden brown from both sides.
3. In a bowl, add all the topping ingredients and mix well.
4. Spoon the topping mixture over bread slices.
5. Serve and enjoy.

102. **Spicy Chicken Burger Patties**

 10 mins   12 mins

 22 mins   6

- 1 lb. (450 g) ground chicken
- 1 tsp. chili powder
- 1 tsp. cayenne powder
- 1 tbsp. honey
- ¼ cup almond flour
- ¼ tsp. pepper
- 2 tsp. dried parsley
- 1 tsp. paprika
- ¼ tsp. salt

1. Add all ingredients into a bowl and mix until well combined.
2. Preheat the grill to high heat.
3. Spray the grill top with cooking spray.
4. Make patties from the mixture and place them on the hot grill top and cook for 4–6 minutes on each side.
5. Serve and enjoy.

Cal: 165kcal | Carb: 3.8g | Fat: 6.4g | Prot: 22.3g | Sugar: 3g | Cholesterol: 67mg

 Cal: 361kcal | Carb: 16.6g | Fat: 27.1g | Prot: 12.7g | Sugar: 2.8g | Cholesterol: 67mg

103. <u>Easy Pepperoni Pizza Sandwich</u>

 10 mins   10 mins

 20 mins   3

- 6 bread slices
- 1 ½ cups mozzarella cheese, shredded
- 3 tbsp. butter
- ¾ cup pizza sauce
- 15 pepperoni slices

1. Spread butter on one side of each bread slice.
2. Take 3 bread slices and spread with marinara sauce and top with pepperoni slices and cheese.
3. Cover with remaining bread slices.
4. Preheat the grill to high heat.
5. Spray grill top with cooking spray.
6. Place sandwiches on a hot grill top and cook for 5 minutes or until lightly golden brown from both sides.

104. <u>Easy Pineapple Slices</u>

 10 mins   12 mins

 22 mins   4

- 4 pineapple slices
- 1 tbsp. butter, melted
- ¼ tsp chili powder
- Salt

1. Preheat the grill to high heat.
2. Brush pineapple slices with butter, chili powder, and salt.
3. Place pineapple slices on a hot grill top and cook for 5-6 minutes on each side.
4. Servings and enjoy.

Cal: 108kcal | Carb: 21.7g | Fat: 3.1g | Prot: 0.9g | Sugar: 16.3g | Cholesterol: 8mg

MARINADES, SAUCE CLASSICS AND SPICY BBQ SAUCES

CHAPTER 9.
MARINADES, SAUCE CLASSICS AND SPICY BBQ SAUCES

105. Mirin and Soy Sauce

 4 mins 0 min

 4 mins 2 cups

- ¾ cup water
- ½ cup mirin
- ½ cup soy sauce
- ¼ cup sesame oil
- 1 tablespoon garlic powder
- 1 tablespoon ground ginger
- 1 Tablespoon Grated Fresh Ginger

1. Put ingredients in a medium bowl and whisk until combined. Use immediately or store refrigerated for up to 10 days.

 Cal: 99kcal | Carb: 0.3g | Fat: 6.4g | Prot: 1.2g | Sugar: 0.3g | Cholesterol: 43mg

106. Sweet & Spicy BBQ Sauce

 5 mins 10 mins

 15 mins 40

- Tomato sauce – 3-½ cups.
- White pepper–½ tsp.
- Red pepper flakes – 1 tsp.
- Ground mustard – 1 tbsp.
- Onion powder – 1 tbsp.
- Garlic powder – 1 tbsp.
- Paprika – 2 tbsps.
- Soy sauce – 3 tbsps.
- Worcestershire sauce – 3 tbsps.
- Molasses –½ cup.
- Brown sugar – 1 cup.

1. Add tomato sauce, soy sauce, Worcestershire sauce, molasses, and brown sugar to a grill and stir well to combine.

2. Add paprika, white pepper, red pepper flakes, ground mustard, onion powder, and garlic powder and stir to combine.
3. Cook sauce over a medium heat. Bring to boil.
4. Turn heat to medium-low and simmer for 5 minutes. Remove grill from heat and let it cool completely.
5. Pour sauce into an air-tight container and store in the refrigerator.

 Cal: 43kcal | Carb: 11g | Fat: 1g | Prot: 1g

107. BBQ White Sauce

 5 mins   10 mins

 15 mins   16

- Mayonnaise – 1-½ cups.
- Horseradish – 2 tsps.
- Worcestershire sauce – 1 tsp.
- Brown sugar – 1 tbsp.
- Spicy brown mustard – 1 tbsp.
- Onion powder –½ tsp.
- Garlic powder –½ tsp.
- Apple cider vinegar – ¼ cup.
- Salt – 1 tsp.

1. Add all ingredients into a mixing bowl and whisk until smooth. Pour sauce into an air-tight container and store in the refrigerator for up to 1 week.

 Cal: 156kcal | Carb: 1g | Fat: 17g | Prot: 1g

108. Perfect Honey BBQ Sauce

 5 mins   15 mins

 20 mins   24

- Ketchup – 1 cup.
- Onion powder – 1 tsp.
- Garlic powder – 1 tsp.
- Smoked paprika – 1 tsp.
- Honey – 2 tbsps.
- Apple cider vinegar –¼ cup.
- Brown sugar –½ cup.
- Black pepper –½ tsp.
- Salt – 1 tsp.

1. Add all ingredients into the grill and heat over a medium heat. Bring to boil. Turn heat to low and simmer for 15 minutes. Remove grill from heat and let it cool completely.

Pour sauce into an air-tight container and store in the refrigerator for up to 2 weeks.

 Cal: 35kcal | Carb: 9g | Fat: 1g | Prot: 1g

109. Mango BBQ Sauce

 5 mins   35 mins

 40 mins   12

- Brown sugar – ½ cup.
- Ground ginger – 1 tbsp.
- Smoked paprika – 1 tbsp.
- Ground mustard – 1 tbsp.
- Chili flakes – 2 tbsps.
- Honey – 3 tbsps.
- Apple cider vinegar – ¾ cup.
- Tomato paste – 6 oz. (170 g)
- Mango – 2 cups, chopped.
- Garlic cloves – 4, chopped.
- Habanero peppers – 4, diced.
- Small onion – 1, chopped.
- Olive oil – 1 tsp.
- Pepper & salt, to taste.

1. Heat olive oil in a grill over a medium heat. Add peppers and onion and sauté for 5 minutes. Add garlic and sauté for a minute.

Add remaining ingredients and stir until well combined. Bring to boil. Turn heat to low and simmer for 20-30 minutes. Remove grill from heat. Puree the sauce until smooth. Pour sauce into an air-tight container and store in the refrigerator.

 Cal: 104kcal | Carb: 23g | Fat: 1g | Prot: 1g

110. Peach BBQ Sauce

 5 mins   20 mins

 25 mins   24

- Ketchup – ¼ cup.
- Liquid smoke – ¼ tsp.
- Dry mustard – ½ tsp.
- Chili powder – 1 tsp.
- Dijon mustard – 1 tbsp.
- Worcestershire sauce – 1 tbsp.
- Balsamic vinegar – 2 tbsps.
- Apple cider vinegar – ¼ cup.
- Soy sauce – ¼ cup.
- Tomato paste – 2 tbsps.
- Honey – 2 tbsps.
- Molasses – 2 tbsps.
- Brown sugar – ¾ cup.
- Water – 1-½ cups.

- Frozen peaches – 1 lb. (450 g)
- Bourbon – 4 tbsps.
- Jalapeno pepper – 2 tbsps., diced.
- Onion – 1 cup, diced.
- Olive oil – 2 tbsps.
- Black pepper – ½ tsp.
- salt – ½ tsp.

1. Heat olive oil in a grill over medium heat.
2. Add jalapeno and onion and sauté for 3-4 minutes.
3. Add bourbon and cook for 1 minute.
4. Add 1 cup water and peaches and cook for 10 minutes. Remove grill from heat.
5. Pour pan contents into the food processor and process until smooth. Return blended mixture to the grill along with remaining ingredients and cook over medium heat for 5 minutes.
6. Remove grill from heat and let it cool completely. Pour sauce into an air-tight container and store in the refrigerator.

 Cal: 55kcal | Carb: 9.6g | Fat: 1.2g | Prot: 0.5g

111. <u>Easy BBQ Sauce</u>

 5 mins   15 mins

 20 mins   10

- Brown sugar – 1-½ cups.
- Onion powder – 2 tsps.
- Paprika – 2 tsps.
- Worcestershire sauce – 1 tbsp.
- Apple cider vinegar – ½ cup.
- Ketchup – 1-½ cups.
- Pepper – 1 tsp.
- salt – 2 tsps.

1. Add all ingredients into a small grill and heat over a medium heat. Bring to boil. Turn heat to low and simmer for 15 minutes. Store and serve.

 Cal: 167kcal | Carb: 43g | Fat: 3.4g | Prot: 1g

SWEET RECIPES

CHAPTER 10.
SWEET RECIPES

112. Spicy Sausage & Cheese Balls

 20 mins   40 mins

 1 h   4

- 1lb Hot Breakfast Sausage
- 2 cups Bisquick Baking Mix
- 8 ounces (230 g) Cream Cheese
- 8 ounces (230 g) Extra Sharp Cheddar Cheese
- ¼ cup Fresno Peppers
- 1 tablespoon Dried Parsley
- 1 teaspoon Killer Hogs AP Rub
- ½ teaspoon Onion Powder

1. Get ready grill or flame broil for roundabout cooking at 400-degrees F.
2. Blend Sausage, Baking Mix, destroyed cheddar, cream cheddar, and remaining fixings in a huge bowl until all-around fused.
3. Utilize a little scoop to parcel blend into chomp to estimate balls and roll tenderly fit as a fiddle.

4. Spot wiener and cheddar balls on a cast-iron container and cook for 15mins.
5. Present with your most loved plunging sauces.

 Cal: 95kcal │ Carb: 4g │ Fat: 7g │ Prot: 5g

113. White Chocolate Bread Pudding

 20 mins   1 h and 15 mins

 1 h and 35 mins   12

- 1 loaf French bread
- 4 cups Heavy Cream
- 3 Large Eggs
- 2 cups White Sugar
- 1 package White Chocolate morsels
- ¼ cup Melted Butter
- 2 teaspoons Vanilla
- 1 teaspoon Ground Nutmeg
- 1 teaspoon Salt
- Bourbon White Chocolate Sauce
- 1 package White Chocolate morsels
- 1 cup Heavy Cream

88

- 2 tablespoons Melted Butter
- 2 tablespoons Bourbon
- ½ teaspoon Salt

1. Preheat the grill at 350-degrees F.
2. Tear French bread into little portions and spot in a massive bowl. Pour four cups of Heavy Cream over Bread and douse for 30mins.
3. Join eggs, sugar, softened spread, and vanilla in a medium to estimate bowl. Include a package of white chocolate pieces and a delicate blend. Season with Nutmeg and Salt.
4. Pour egg combo over the splashed French bread and blend to sign up for.
5. Pour the combination right into a properly to buttered 9 x 13 to inch meal dish and spot it at the grill.
6. Cook for 60 Secs or until bread pudding has set and the top is darker.
7. For the sauce: Melt margarine in a saucepot over medium warm temperature. Add whiskey and hold on cooking for three to 4mins until liquor vanished and margarine begins to darkish-colored.
8. Include vast cream and heat till a mild stew. Take from the warmth and consist of white chocolate pieces a bit at a time continuously blending until the complete percent has softened. Season with a hint of salt and serve over bread pudding.

 Cal: 372kcal | Carb: 31g | Fat: 25g | Prot: 5g

114. **Cheesy Jalapeño Grill Dip**

 10 mins   15 mins

 25 mins   8

- 8 ounces (230 g) cream cheese
- 16 ounces (450 g) shredded cheese
- ⅓ cup mayonnaise
- 4 ounces (110 g) diced green chilies
- 3 fresh jalapeños
- 2 teaspoons Killer Hogs AP Rub
- 2 teaspoons Mexican Style Seasoning

For the topping:
- ¼ cup Mexican Blend Shredded Cheese
- Sliced jalapeños
- Mexican Style Seasoning
- 3 tablespoons Killer Hogs AP Rub
- 2 tablespoons Chili Powder
- 2 tablespoons Paprika
- 2 teaspoons Cumin
- ½ teaspoon Granulated Onion
- ¼ teaspoon Cayenne Pepper
- ¼ teaspoon Chipotle Chili Pepper ground
- ¼ teaspoon Oregano

1. Preheat grill or flame broil for roundabout cooking at 350 degrees

2. Join fixings in a big bowl and spot in a cast to press grill
3. Top with Mexican Blend destroyed cheddar and cuts of jalapeno's
4. Spot iron grill on flame broil mesh and cook until cheddar hot and bubbly and the top has seared
5. Marginally about 25 mins.
6. Serve warm with enormous corn chips (scoops), tortilla chips, or your preferred vegetables for plunging.

 Cal: 150kcal | Carb: 22g | Fat: 6g | Prot: 3g

115. <u>Cajun Turkey Club</u>

 5 mins   10 mins

 15 mins   3

- 1 3lbs Turkey Breast
- 1 stick Butter (melted)
- 8 ounces (230 g) Chicken Broth
- 1 tablespoon Killer Hogs Hot Sauce
- ¼ cup Malcolm's King Craw Seasoning
- 8 Pieces to Thick Sliced Bacon
- 1 cup Brown Sugar
- 1 head Green Leaf Lettuce
- 1 Tomato (sliced)

- 6 slices Toasted Bread
- ½ cup Cajun Mayo
- 1 cup Mayo
- 1 tablespoon Dijon Mustard
- 1 tablespoon Killer Hogs Sweet Fire Pickles (chopped)
- 1 tablespoon Horseradish
- ½ teaspoon Malcolm's King Craw Seasoning
- 1 teaspoon Killer Hogs Hot Sauce
- Pinch of Salt & Black Pepper to taste

1. Preheat the grill 325-degrees F
2. Join dissolved margarine, chicken stock, hot sauce, and 1 tbsp. of Cajun Seasoning in a blending bowl. Infuse the blend into the turkey bosom scattering the infusion destinations for even inclusion.
3. Clean the outside of the turkey breast with a vegetable cooking splash and season it with the Malcom's King Craw Seasoning.
4. Spot the turkey bosom on the grill and cook until the inside temperature arrives at 165 degrees. Utilize a moment read thermometer to screen temp during the cooking procedure.
5. Consolidate darker sugar and 1 teaspoon of King Craw in a little bowl. Spread the bacon with the sugar blend and spot on a cooling rack.
6. Cook the bacon for 12 to 15mins or until darker. Make certain to turn the bacon part of the way through for cooking.
7. Toast the bread, cut the tomatoes dainty, and wash/dry the lettuce leaves.
8. At the point when the turkey bosom arrives at 165 take it from the flame broil and rest for 15mins. Take the netting out from around the bosom and cut into slender cuts.
9. To cause the sandwich: To slather Cajun Mayo* on the toast, stack on a few cuts of turkey bosom, lettuce, tomato, and bacon. Include another bit of toast and rehash a similar procedure. Include the top bit of toast slathered with more Cajun mayo, cut the sandwich into equal parts and appreciate.

Cal: 130kcal | Carb: 1g | Fat: 4g | Prot: 21g

116. **Juicy Loosey Cheeseburger**

 10 mins   10 mins

 20 mins   6

- 2 lbs. ground beef
- 1 egg beaten
- 1 Cup dry bread crumbs
- 3 tablespoons evaporated milk
- 2 tablespoons Worcestershire sauce
- 1 tablespoon Grill Grills All Purpose Rub
- 4 slices of cheddar cheese
- 4 buns

1. Start by consolidating the hamburger, egg, dissipated milk, Worcestershire and focus on a bowl. Utilize your hands to blend well. Partition this blend into 4 equivalent parts. At that point take every one of the 4 sections and partition them into equal parts. Take every one of these little parts and smooth them. The objective is to have 8 equivalent level patties that you will at that point join into 4 burgers.

2. When you have your patties smoothed, place your cheddar in the center and afterward place the other patty over this and firmly squeeze the sides to seal. You may even need to push the meat back towards the inside a piece to shape a marginally thicker patty. The patties ought to be marginally bigger than a standard burger bun as they will recoil a bit of during cooking.

3. Preheat your Kong to 300 degrees.

4. Keep in mind during flame broiling that you fundamentally have two meager patties, one on each side, so the cooking time ought not to have a place. You will cook these for 5 to 8mins per side—closer to 5mins on the off chance that you favor an uncommon burger or more towards 8mins if you like a well to done burger.

5. At the point when you flip the burgers, take a toothpick and penetrate the focal point of the burger to permit steam to getaway. This will shield you from having a hit to out or having a visitor who gets a jaw consume from liquid cheddar as they take their first nibble.

6. Toss these on a pleasant roll and top with fixings that supplement whatever your burgers are loaded down with.

 Cal: 300kcal | Carb: 33g | Fat: 12g | Prot: 15g

117. <u>No Flip Burgers</u>

 30 mins   30 mins

 1 h   2

- Ground Beef Patties
- Grill Grills Beef Rub
- Choice of Cheese
- Choice of Toppings
- Pretzel Buns

1. To start, you'll need to begin with freezing yet not solidified meat patties. This will help guarantee that you don't overcook your burgers. Liberally sprinkle on our Beef Rub or All to Purpose Rub and delicately knead into the two sides of the patty. As another option, you can likewise season with salt and pepper and some garlic salt.
2. Preheat your grill to 250-degrees Fahrenheit and cook for about 45 mins. Contingent upon the thickness of your burgers you will need to keep an eye on them after around 30 to 45 mins, yet there's no compelling reason to flip. For a medium to uncommon burger, we recommend cooking to about 155 degrees.
3. After the initial 30 to 40 mins, if you like liquefied cheddar on your burger feel free to mix it up. Close your barbecue back up and

let them wrap up for another 10 mins before evacuating. For an additional punch of flavor, finish your burger off with a sprinkle of Grill Grill's Gold 'N Bold sauce. Appreciate.

 Cal: 190kcal | Carb: 17g | Fat: 9g | Prot: 13g

118. <u>Bread Pudding</u>

 15 mins   45 mins

 1 h   4

- 8 stale donuts
- 3 eggs
- 1 cup milk
- 1 cup heavy cream
- ½ cup brown sugar
- 1 teaspoon vanilla
- 1 pinch salt
- Blueberry Compote
- 1-pint blueberries
- ⅔ cup granulated sugar
- ¼ cup water
- 1 lemon
- Oat Topping
- 1 cup quick oats
- ½ cup brown sugar

- 1 teaspoon flour
- 2 to 3 tablespoons room temperature butter

1. Warmth your Grill to 350 degrees.
2. Cut your doughnuts into 6 pieces for every doughnut and put it in a safe spot. Blend your eggs, milk, cream, darker sugar, vanilla, and salt in a bowl until it's everything fused. Spot your doughnuts in a lubed 9 by 13 containers at that point pour your custard blend over the doughnuts. Press down on the doughnuts to guarantee they get covered well and absorb the juices.
3. In another bowl, consolidate your oats, dark colored sugar, flour and gradually join the spread with your hand until the blend begins to cluster up like sand. When that is Prepared, sprinkle it over the highest point of the bread pudding and toss it on the barbecue around 40 to 45mins until it gets decent and brilliant dark colored.
4. While the bread pudding is Prepared, place your blueberries into a grill over medium-high warmth and begin to cook them down so the juices begin to stream. When that occurs, include your sugar and water and blend well. Diminish the warmth to drug low and let it cool down until it begins to thicken up. Right when the blend begins to thicken, pizzazz your lemon and add the get-up-and-go to the blueberry compote and afterward cut your lemon down the middle and squeeze it into the blend. What you're left with is a tasty, splendid compote that is ideal for the sweetness of the bread pudding.
5. Watch out for your bread pudding around the 40 to 50mins mark. The blend will, in any case, shake a piece in the middle however will solidify as it stands once you pull it off. You can pull it early on the off chance that you like your bread pudding more sodden however to me, the ideal bread pudding will be dimmer with some caramelization yet will at present have dampness too!
6. Presently this is the point at which I'd snatch an attractive bowl, toss a pleasant aiding of bread pudding in there then top it off with the compote and a stacking scoop of vanilla

bean frozen yogurt at that point watch faces light up. In addition to the fact that this is an amazingly beautiful dish, the flavor will take you out. Destined to be an enormous hit in your family unit. Give it a shot and express gratitude toward me.

7. What's more, as usual, ensure you snap a photo of your manifestations and label us in your dishes! We'd love to include your work.

 Cal: 290kcal | Carb: 62g | Fat: 4g | Prot: 5g

119. <u>Smoked Chocolate Bacon Pecan Pie</u>

 1 h and 45 mins   45 mins

 2 h and 30 mins   8

- 4 eggs
- 1 cup chopped pecans
- 1 tablespoon of vanilla
- ½ cup semi to sweet chocolate chips
- ½ cup dark corn syrup
- ½ cup light corn syrup
- ¾ cup bacon (crumbled)
- ¼ cup bourbon
- 4 tablespoons or ¼ cup of butter
- ½ cup brown sugar

- ½ cup white sugar
- 1 tablespoon cornstarch
- 1 package refrigerated pie dough
- 16 ounces (450 g) heavy cream
- ¾ cup white sugar
- ¼ cup bacon
- 1 tablespoon vanilla

1. Pie:
2. Carry Grill to 350 degrees.
3. Blend 4 tablespoons spread, ½ cup darker sugar, and ½ cup white sugar in blending bowl.
4. In a different bowl, blend 4 eggs and 1 tablespoon cornstarch together and add to blender.
5. Include ½ cup dull corn syrup, ½ cup light corn syrup, ¼ cup whiskey, 1 cup slashed walnuts, 1 cup bacon, and 1 tablespoon vanilla to blend.
6. Spot pie batter in 9-inch (22,9 cm) pie grill.
7. Daintily flour mixture.
8. Uniformly place ½ cup chocolate contributes pie dish.
9. Take blend into the pie dish.
10. Smoke at 350 degrees for 40mins or until the focus is firm.
11. Cool and top with bacon whipped cream.
12. Bacon whipped Cream:
13. Consolidate fixings (16 ounces (450 g) substantial cream, ¾ cup white sugar, ¼ cup bacon to finely cleaved, and 1 tablespoon vanilla) and mix at rapid until blend thickens. This formula can be separated into 6mins pie container or custard dishes or filled in as one entire pie.

Cal: 200kcal | Carb: 18g | Fat: 0g | Prot: 3g

120. **Bacon Sweet Potato Pie**

 15 mins   50 mins

 1 h and 5 mins   8

- 1 pound 3 ounces (540 g) sweet potatoes
- 1 ¼ cups plain yogurt
- ¾ cup packed, dark brown sugar
- ½ teaspoon of cinnamon
- ¼ teaspoon of nutmeg
- 5 egg yolks
- ¼ teaspoon of salt
- 1 (up to 9 inch (22,9 cm)) deep dish, frozen pie shell
- 1 cup chopped pecans, toasted
- 4 strips of bacon, cooked and diced
- 1 tablespoon maple syrup
- Optional: Whipped topping

1. In the first region, 3D shapes the potatoes right into a steamer crate and sees into a good-sized pot of stew water. Ensure the water is not any nearer than creeps from the base of the bushel. When steamed for 20mins, pound with a potato masher and installed a safe spot.
2. While your flame broil is preheating, location the sweet potatoes within the bowl of a stand blender and beat with the oar connection.

3. Include yogurt, dark colored sugar, cinnamon, nutmeg, yolks, and salt, to flavor, and beat until very a whole lot joined. Take this hitter into the pie shell and see onto a sheet dish. Sprinkle walnuts and bacon on pinnacle and bathe with maple syrup.
4. Heat for 45 to 60mins or until the custard arrives at 165 to 180 degrees. Take out from fish fry and funky. Keep refrigerated within the wake of cooling.

 Cal: 270kcal | Carb: 39g | Fat: 12g | Prot: 4g

121. **Grill Fruit with Cream**

 15 mins   10 mins

 25 mins   6

- 2 halved Apricot
- 1 halved Nectarine
- 2 halved peaches
- ¼ cup of Blueberries
- ½ cup of Raspberries
- 2 tablespoons of Honey
- 1 orange{ XE "oranges" }, the peel
- 2 cups of Cream
- ½ cup of Balsamic Vinegar

1. Preheat the grill to 400F with closed lid.
2. Grill the peaches, nectarines and apricots for 4 minutes on each side.
3. Place a pan over the stove and turn on medium heat. Add 2 tablespoons of honey, vinegar, and orange{ XE "oranges" } peel. Simmer until medium thick.
4. In the meantime, add honey and cream in a bowl. Whip until it reaches a soft form.
5. Place the fruits on a serving plate. Sprinkle with berries. Drizzle with balsamic reduction. Serve with cream and enjoy!

 Cal: 230kcal | Carb: 35g | Fat: 3g | Prot: 3g

122. **Grill Layered Cake**

 10 mins   20 mins

 30 mins   6

- 2 x pound (910 g) cake
- 3 cups of whipped cream
- ¼ cup melted butter
- 1 cup of blueberries
- 1 cup of raspberries
- 1 cup sliced strawberries

1. Preheat the grill to high with closed lid.
2. Slice the cake loaf (¾ inch (1,9 cm)), about 10 per loaf. Brush both sides with butter.
3. Grill for 7 minutes on each side. Set aside.
4. Once cooled completely start layering your cake. Place cake, berries then cream.
5. Sprinkle with berries and serve.

 Cal: 160kcal | Carb: 22g | Fat: 6g | Prot: 2.3g

123. <u>Coconut Chocolate Simple Brownies</u>

 15 mins   25 mins

 40 mins   6

- 4 eggs
- 1 cup Cane Sugar
- ¾ cup of Coconut oil
- 4 ounces (110 g) chocolate, chopped
- ½ teaspoon of Sea salt
- ¼ cup cocoa powder, unsweetened
- ½ cup flour
- 4 ounces (110 g) Chocolate chips
- 1 teaspoon of Vanilla

1. Preheat the grill to 350F with closed lid.
2. Take a baking pan (9x9), grease it and line a parchment paper.
3. In a bowl combine the salt, cocoa powder and flour. Stir and set aside.
4. In the microwave or double boiler melt the coconut oil and chopped chocolate. Let it cool a bit.
5. Add the vanilla, eggs, and sugar. Whisk to combine.
6. Add into the flour, and add chocolate chips. Pour the mixture into a pan.
7. Place the pan on the grate. Bake for 20 minutes. If you want dryer brownies to bake for 5 - 10 minutes more.
8. Let them cool before cutting.
9. Cut the brownies into squares and serve.

 Cal: 135kcal | Carb: 16g | Fat: 3g | Prot: 2g

124. <u>Bacon Chocolate Chip Cookies</u>

 30 mins   30 mins

 1 h   6

- 8 slices cooked and crumbled bacon

- 2 ½ teaspoon apple cider vinegar
- 1 teaspoon vanilla
- 2 cup semisweet chocolate chips
- 2 room temp eggs
- 1 ½ teaspoon baking soda
- 1 cup granulated sugar
- ½ teaspoon salt
- 2 ¾ cup all-purpose flour
- 1 cup light brown sugar
- 1 ½ stick softened butter

1. Mix salt, baking soda and flour.
2. Cream the sugar and the butter together. Lower the speed. Add in the eggs, vinegar, and vanilla.
3. Put it on low fire, slowly add in the flour mixture, bacon pieces, and chocolate chips.
4. Preheat your grill, with your lid closed, until it reaches 375.
5. Put a parchment paper on a baking sheet you are using and drop a teaspoonful of cookie batter on the baking sheet. Let them cook on the grill, covered, for approximately 12 minutes or until they are browned.

 Cal: 167kcal | Carb: 21g | Fat: 9g | Prot: 2g

125. <u>**Chocolate Chip Cookies**</u>

 30 mins   30 mins

 1 h   8

- 1 ½ cup chopped walnuts
- 1 teaspoon vanilla
- 2 cup chocolate chips
- 1 teaspoon baking soda
- 2 ½ cup plain flour
- ½ teaspoon salt
- 1 ½ stick softened butter
- 2 eggs
- 1 cup brown sugar
- ½ cup sugar

1. Preheat your grill, with your lid closed, until it reaches 350.
2. Mix the baking soda, salt, and flour.
3. Cream the brown sugar, sugar, and butter. Mix in the vanilla and eggs until it comes together.
4. Slowly add in the flour while continuing to beat. Once all flour has been incorporated, add in the chocolate chips and walnuts. Using a spoon, fold into batter.
5. Place an aluminum foil onto grill. In an aluminum foil, drop spoonful of dough and bake for 17 minutes.

Cal: 150kcal | Carb: 18g | Fat: 5g | Prot: 10g

126. Apple Cobbler

 Cal: 152kcal | Carb: 26g | Fat: 5g | Prot: 1g

127. Cinnamon Sugar Pumpkin Seeds

 30 mins   1 h and 50 mins

 2 h and 20 mins   8

- 8 Granny Smith apples
- 1 cup sugar
- 1 stick melted butter
- 1teaspoon cinnamon
- Pinch salt
- ½ cup brown sugar
- 2 eggs
- 2 teaspoons baking powder
- 2 cup plain flour
- 1 ½ cup sugar

1. Peel and quarter apples, place into a bowl. Add in the cinnamon and one c. sugar. Stir well to coat and let it set for one hour.
2. Preheat your grill, with your lid closed, until it reaches 350.
3. In a large bowl add the salt, baking powder, eggs, brown sugar, sugar, and flour. Mix until it forms crumbles.
4. Place apples into rack add the crumble mixture on top and drizzle with melted butter.
5. Place on the grill and cook for 50 minutes.

 15 mins   30 mins

 45 mins   8

- 2 tablespoons sugar
- Seeds from a pumpkin
- 1 teaspoon cinnamon
- 2 tablespoons melted butter

1. Preheat your grill, with your lid closed, until it reaches 350.
2. Clean the seeds and toss them in the melted butter. Add them to the sugar and cinnamon. Spread them out on a baking sheet, place on the grill for 25 minutes. Serve.

 Cal: 127kcal | Carb: 15g | Fat: 21g | Prot: 5g

128. <u>Blackberry Pie</u>

 15 mins 40 mins

 55 mins 8

- Butter, for greasing
- ½ cup all-purpose flour
- ½ cup milk
- 2 pints blackberries
- 2 cup sugar, divided
- 1 box refrigerated piecrusts
- 1 stick melted butter
- 1 stick of butter
- Vanilla ice cream

1. Preheat your grill, with your lid closed, until it reaches 375 F.
2. Butter a cast iron grill.
3. Unroll a piecrust and lay it in the bottom and up the sides of the grill. Use a fork to poke holes in the crust.
4. Lay the grill and grill for five mins, or until the crust is browned. Set off the grill.
5. Mix together 1 ½ c. of sugar, flour and melted butter together. Add in the blackberries and toss everything together.
6. The berry mixture should be added to the grill. The milk should be added on the top afterward. Sprinkle on half of the diced butter.
7. Unroll the second pie crust and lay it over the grill. You can also slice it into strips and weave it on top to make it look like a lattice. Place the rest of the diced butter over the top. Sprinkle the rest of the sugar over the crust and place it grill back on the grill.
8. Lower the lid and smoke for 15 to 20 minutes or until it is browned and bubbly. You may want to cover with some foil to keep it from burning during the last few minutes of cooking. Serve the hot pie with some vanilla ice cream.

Cal: 393kcal │ Carb: 53.7g │ Fat: 18.8g │ Prot: 4.3g

129. <u>S'mores Dip</u>

 10 mins 25 mins

 35 mins 8

- 12 ounces (340 g) semisweet chocolate chips
- ¼ cup milk
- 2 tablespoons melted salted butter
- 16 ounces (450 g) marshmallows
- Apple wedges
- Graham crackers

1. Preheat your grill, with your lid closed, until it reaches 450.
2. Put a cast iron grill on your grill and add in the milk and melted butter. Stir together for a minute.
3. Once it has heated up, top with the chocolate chips, making sure it makes a single layer. Place the marshmallows on top, standing them on their end and covering the chocolate.
4. Cover, and let it smoke for five to seven minutes. The marshmallows should be toasted lightly.
5. Take the grill off the heat and serve with apple wedges and graham crackers.

 Cal: 217kcal | Carb: 41g | Fat: 4.7g | Prot: 2.7g

130. Ice Cream Bread

 10 mins   1 h

  1 h and 10 mins   6

- 1 ½ quart full-fat butter pecan ice cream, softened
- 1 teaspoon salt
- 2 cups semisweet chocolate chips
- 1 cup sugar
- 1 stick melted butter
- Butter, for greasing
- 4 cups self-rising flour

1. Preheat your grill, with your lid closed, until it reaches 350.
2. Mix together the salt, sugar, flour, and ice cream with an electric mixer set to medium for two minutes.
3. As the mixer is still running, add in the chocolate chips, beating until everything is blended.
4. Spray a Bundt pan or tube pan with cooking spray. If you choose to use a pan that is solid, the center will take too long to cook. That's why a tube or Bundt pan works best.
5. Add the butter to your prepared pan.
6. Set the cake on the grill, cover, and smoke for 50 minutes to an hour. A toothpick should come out clean.
7. Take the pan off of the grill. For 10 minutes cool the bread. Remove carefully the bread from the pan and then drizzle it with some melted butter.

Cal: 149kcal | Carb: 27g | Fat: 3g | Prot: 3.5g

SIDES AND SALADS

CHAPTER 11.
SIDES AND SALADS

131. Brisket Baked Beans

 20 mins   1 h

 1 h and 20 mins   10-12

- 2 tablespoons extra virgin olive oil
- 1 large, diced onion
- 1 diced green pepper
- 1 red pepper diced
- 2-6 jalapeño peppers diced
- 3 pieces Texas-style brisket flat chopped
- 1 (28 oz. (790 g)) baked beans, like Bush's country-style baked beans
- 1 (28 oz. (790 g)) pork and beans
- 1 (14 oz. (400 g)) red kidney beans, rinse, drain
- 1 cup barbecue sauce like Sweet Baby Ray's barbecue sauce
- ½ cup stuffed brown sugar
- 3 garlics, chopped
- 2 teaspoons of mustard
- ½ teaspoon salt
- ½ teaspoon black pepper

1. Heat the olive oil in a skillet over medium heat and add the diced onion, peppers, and jalapeño. Cook, occasionally stirring, for about 8-10 minutes until the onion is translucent.
2. In a 4-quart casserole dish, mix chopped brisket, baked beans, pork beans, kidney beans, cooked onions, peppers, barbecue sauce, brown sugar, garlic, mustard, salt, and black pepper.
3. Configure a grill for indirect cooking and preheat to 325 °F (160 °C) . Cook the beans baked in the brisket for 1.5 to 2 hours until they become bare beans. Rest for 15 minutes before eating.

 Cal: 264kcal | Carb: 35g | Fat: 8g | Prot: 15g | Saturated Fat: 2g

132. Bacon Cheddar Slider

 30 mins   15 mins

 45 mins   6-10 (1-2 sliders each as an appetizer)

- 1-pound (450 g) ground beef (80% lean)
- ½ teaspoon of garlic salt
- ½ teaspoon salt
- ½ teaspoon of garlic
- ½ teaspoon onion
- ½ teaspoon black pepper
- 6 bacon slices, cut in half
- ½ cup mayonnaise
- 6 (1 oz. (28 g)) sliced sharp cheddar cheese, cut in half (optional)
- 1 Sliced red onion
- 12 mini breads, sliced horizontally
- Ketchup

1. Place ground beef, garlic salt, seasoned salt, garlic powder, onion powder, and black pepper in a medium bowl.
2. Divide the meat mixture into 12 equal parts, shape into small thin round patties (about 2 ounces (57 g) each) and save.
3. Cook the bacon on medium heat over medium heat for 5-8 minutes until crunchy. Set aside.
4. To make the sauce, mix the mayonnaise and horseradish in a small bowl if using.
5. Set up a grill for direct cooking to use grill accessories. Contact the manufacturer to see if there is a grill accessory that works with the grill.
6. Spray a cooking spray on the grill cooking surface for best nonstick results.
7. Preheat grill to 350 °F (180 °C) . The grill surface should be approximately 400 °F (200 °C) .
8. Grill the putty for 3-4 minutes each until the internal temperature reaches 160 °F (70 °C) .
9. If necessary, place a sharp cheddar cheese slice on each patty while it is on the grill or after the patty is removed from the grill. Place a small amount of mayonnaise mixture, a slice of red onion, and a hamburger pate in the lower half of each roll. Pickled slices, bacon, and ketchup.

 Cal: 335kcal | Carb: 0g | Fat: 29g | Prot: 78g | Saturated Fat: 10g

133. Grilled Mushroom Skewers

 5 mins   1 h

 1 h and 5 mins   6

- 16 oz. 1 lb. (900 g) baby portobello mushrooms
- For the marinade:
- ¼ cup olive oil
- ¼ cup lemon juice
- A small handful parsley
- 1 teaspoon sugar
- 1 teaspoon salt
- ¼ teaspoon pepper
- ¼ teaspoon cayenne pepper
- 1 to 2 garlic cloves
- 1 tablespoon balsamic vinegar
- What you will need:
- 10-inch (25,4 cm) bamboo/wood skewers

1. Spot 10 medium sticks into a heating dish and spread with water. It's critical to douse the sticks for in any event 15 minutes (more

is better), or they will consume too rapidly on the flame broil.

2. Spot most of the marinade fixings in a nourishment processor and heartbeat a few times until the marinade is almost smooth.

3. Flush your mushrooms and pat dry. Cut each mushroom down the middle, so each piece has half of the mushroom stem.

4. Spot the mushroom parts into an enormous gallon-size Ziploc sack or a medium bowl and pour in the marinade. Shake the pack until most of the mushrooms are equally covered in marinade. Refrigerate and marinate for 30mins to 45mins.

5. Preheat your barbecue about 300 °F (150 °C).

6. Stick the mushrooms cozily onto the bamboo/wooden sticks that have been dousing (no compelling reason to dry the sticks). Piercing the mushrooms was a bit of irritating from the outset until I got the hang of things.

7. I've discovered that it's least demanding to stick them by bending them onto the stick. If you simply drive the stick through, it might make the mushroom break.

8. Spot the pierced mushrooms on the hot barbecue for around 3mins for every side, causing sure the mushrooms don't consume to the flame broil. The mushrooms are done when they are delicate, as mushrooms ought to be removed from the barbecue. Spread with foil to keep them warm until prepared to serve.

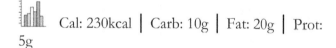 Cal: 230kcal | Carb: 10g | Fat: 20g | Prot: 5g

134. **Caprese Tomato Salad**

 5 mins   1 h

 1 h and 5 mins   4

- 3 cups halved multicolored cherry tomatoes
- 1/8 teaspoon salt
- ½ cup fresh basil leaves
- 1 tablespoon extra-virgin olive oil
- 1 tablespoon balsamic vinegar
- ½ teaspoon black pepper
- ¼ teaspoon salt
- 1 ounce (28 g) diced fresh mozzarella cheese (about ⅓ cup)

1. Join tomatoes and 1/8 teaspoon legitimate salt in an enormous bowl. Let stand 5mins. Include basil leaves, olive oil, balsamic vinegar, pepper, ¼ teaspoon fit salt, and mozzarella; toss.

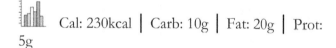 Cal: 80kcal | Carb: 5g | Fat: 5.8g | Prot: 2g | Sugar: 4g

135. Fresh Creamed Corn

 5 mins   30 mins

 35 mins   4

- 2 teaspoons unsalted butter
- 2 cups fresh corn kernels
- 2 tablespoons minced shallots
- ¾ cup 1% low-fat milk
- 2 teaspoons all-purpose flour
- ¼ teaspoon salt

1. Melt butter in a huge nonstick skillet over medium-excessive warmness.
2. Add corn and minced shallots to pan, stirring constantly.
3. Add milk, flour, and salt to pan; bring to a boil.
4. Reduce warmness to low; cover and cook dinner for 4 minutes.

 Cal: 107kcal | Carb: 18g | Fat: 3.4g | Prot: 4g

136. Crunchy Zucchini Chips

 15 mins   25 mins

 40 mins   4

- ⅓ cup whole-wheat panko
- 3 tablespoons uncooked amaranth
- ½ teaspoon garlic powder
- ¼ teaspoon salt
- ¼ teaspoon freshly ground black pepper
- 1-ounce (28 g) parmesan cheese, finely grated
- 12-ounces (340 g) zucchini, cut into ¼ inch (0,6 cm) -thick slices
- 1 tablespoon olive oil
- Cooking spray

1. Preheat stove to 425 °F. Join the initial 6 ingredients in a shallow dish. Join zucchini and oil in an enormous bowl; toss well to coat. Dip zucchini in panko blend, squeeze gently. Put the zucchini on an ovenproof wire rack on a preparing sheet. Heat at 425 °F for 26 minutes or until cooked and fresh. Serve chips right away.

 Cal: 132kcal | Carb: 14g | Fat: 6.5g | Prot: 6g | Sugar: 2g

137. <u>Grilled Green Onions and Orzo and Sweet Peas</u>

 5 mins   15 mins

 20 mins   4

- ¾ cup whole-wheat orzo
- 1 cup frozen peas
- 1 bunch green onions, trimmed
- 1 teaspoon olive oil
- ½ teaspoon grated lemon rind
- 1 tablespoon lemon juice
- ¼ teaspoon salt
- 1 ounce (28 g) shaved Manchego cheese

1. Plan orzo as indicated by way of headings, discarding salt, and fat. Include peas throughout the most recent 2 mins of cooking.
2. Warm a fish fry skillet on high temperature and then toss 1 teaspoon of olive oil on the onions. Cook each surface of the skillet for 2 minutes. Cut the onions and mix them with orzo, lemon skin and juice, 1 teaspoon of olive oil and salt; toss. After that, sprinkle with shaved Manchego cheddar.

 Cal: 197kcal | Fat: 5.6g | Sodium: 204mg

138. <u>Cinnamon Almonds</u>

 10 mins   1 h and 30 mins

 1 h and 40 mins   4 to 6

- 1 egg white
- 1 lb. (450 g) almonds
- ½ cup brown sugar
- ½ cup granulated sugar
- 1/8 teaspoon salt
- 1 tablespoon ground cinnamon

1. Whisk the egg white until frothy. Add the salt, cinnamon, and sugars. Add the almonds and toss to coat.
2. Spread the almonds on a baking dish lined with parchment paper.
3. Preheat the grill to 225 °F with a closed lid.
4. Grill for 1 hour and 30 minutes. Stir often.
5. Serve slightly cooled and enjoy!

 Cal: 280kcal | Carb: 38g | Fat: 13g | Prot: 10g

139. Cranberry-Almond Broccoli Salad

 10 mins   1 h

 1 h and 10 mins   8

- ¼ cup finely chopped red onion
- ⅓ cup canola mayonnaise
- 3 tablespoons 2% reduced-fat Greek yogurt
- 1 tablespoon cider vinegar
- 1 tablespoon honey
- ¼ teaspoon salt
- ¼ teaspoon freshly ground black pepper
- 4 cups coarsely chopped broccoli florets
- ⅓ cup slivered almonds, toasted
- ⅓ cup reduced-sugar dried cranberries
- 4 center-cut bacon slices, cooked and crumbled

1. Absorb red onion cold water for 5 minutes.
2. Consolidate mayonnaise with the following 5 ingredients, blending gently with a whisk. Mix in red onion, broccoli, and remaining ingredients. Spread and chill 1 hour before serving.

 Cal: 104kcal | Carb: 11g | Fat: 5.9g | Prot: 1.8g | Sugar: 5g

140. Grilled Carrots

 5 mins   20 mins

 25 mins   6

- 1 lb. (450 g) carrots, large
- ½ tablespoon salt
- 6 oz. (170 g) butter
- ½ tablespoon black pepper
- Fresh thyme

1. Thoroughly wash the carrots and do not peel. Pat them dry and coat with olive oil.
2. Add salt to your carrots.
3. Meanwhile, preheat a grill to 350 °F.
4. Now place your carrots directly on the grill or on a raised rack.
5. Close and cook for about 20 minutes.
6. While carrots cook, cook butter in a saucepan, small, over medium heat until browned. Stir constantly to avoid it from burning. Remove from heat.
7. Remove carrots from the grill onto a plate, then drizzle with browned butter.
8. Add pepper and splash with thyme.
9. Serve and enjoy.

Cal: 250kcal | Carb: 4g | Fat: 25g | Prot: 1g | Saturated Fat: 15g | Sugar: 3g | Fiber: 2g | Sodium: 402mg | Potassium: 369mg

141. Grilled Brussels sprouts

 15 mins   20 mins

 35 mins   8

- ½ lb. (230 g) bacon, grease reserved
- 1 lb. (450 g) Brussels sprouts
- ½ tablespoon pepper
- ½ tablespoon salt

1. Cook bacon until crispy on a stovetop, reserve its grease, and then chop into small pieces.
2. Meanwhile, wash the Brussels sprouts, trim off the dry end, and remove dried leaves, if any. Half them and set aside.
3. Place ¼ cup reserved grease in a pan, cast-iron, over medium-high heat.
4. Season the Brussels sprouts with pepper and salt.
5. Brown the sprouts on the pan with the cut side down for about 3-4 minutes.
6. In the meantime, preheat your pellet grill to 350-375°F.
7. Place bacon pieces and browned sprouts into your grill-safe pan.
8. Cook for about 20 minutes.
9. Serve immediately.

 Cal: 153kcal | Carb: 3g | Fat: 10g | Prot: 11g | Saturated Fat: 3g | Sugar: 1g | Fiber: 2g | Sodium: 622mg | Potassium: 497mg

GRILL DESSERTS & GRILLED SMOOTHIES

CHAPTER 12.
GRILL DESSERTS & GRILLED SMOOTHIES

142. Bourbon Cocktail with Grill Blood Orange

 6 mins　　 5 mins

 11 mins　　 4

- 4 blood oranges
- ¾ cup bourbon
- 1 tablespoon sugar, plus more for rimming the glasses

1. Preheat grill to medium-high heat and brush with olive oil. Cut 3 of the oranges in half and grill, cut side down, over high heat until charred.
2. Halve the remaining orange, cut into thick slices, and grill until charred on both sides; set aside. Squeeze the orange halves to get 1 cup of juice.
3. Add the juice, bourbon, and sugar to a cocktail shaker. Add ice to fill the shaker almost to the rim. Shake well for about 30

seconds to ensure the sugar dissolves and the drink is well chilled.
4. Strain into a sugar-rimmed coupe or martini glasses and garnish each with a charred orange slice.

 Cal: 120kcal | Carb: 30g | Fat: 0g | Prot: 0g

143. Cheese Blueberry Smoothie

 5 mins　　 5 mins

 10 mins　　 1

- 1 cup unsweetened almond milk
- ½ cup ice
- ¼ tsp vanilla
- 5 drops liquid stevia
- 1 scoop vanilla protein powder
- ⅓ cup blueberries
- 2 oz. (57 g) cream cheese

1. Add all ingredients into the blender and blend until smooth.
2. Serve and enjoy.

 Cal: 380kcal | Carb: 11.1g | Fat: 23.5g | Prot: 5.3g | Cholesterol: 32.7g

144. **Delicious Cinnamon Smoothie**

 5 mins   5 mins

 10 mins   1

- ¼ cup vanilla protein powder
- 1 tbsp. ground chia seeds
- ½ tsp cinnamon
- 1 tbsp. coconut oil
- ½ cup water
- ¼ cup ice
- ½ cup unsweetened coconut milk

1. Add all ingredients into the blender and blend until smooth.
2. Serve and enjoy.

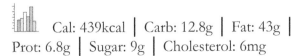 Cal: 439kcal | Carb: 12.8g | Fat: 43g | Prot: 6.8g | Sugar: 9g | Cholesterol: 6mg

145. **Tasty Berry Smoothie**

 5 mins   5 mins

 10 mins   4

- ½ cup blackberries
- ⅔ cup strawberries
- ⅔ cup raspberries
- 1 ½ cups unsweetened almond milk
- ½ cup unsweetened coconut milk
- 1 tbsp. heavy cream

1. Add all ingredients into the blender and blend until smooth.
2. Serve and enjoy.

Cal: 123kcal | Carb: 8.5g | Fat: 10.1g | Prot: 1.8g | Sugar: 4g | Cholesterol: 5mg

146. Healthy Green Smoothie

 5 mins   5 mins

 10 mins   2

- 1 cup avocado
- ½ lemon, peeled
- 1 cucumber, peeled
- 1 tsp ginger, peeled
- ½ cup cilantro
- 1 cup baby spinach
- 1 cup of water

1. Add all ingredients into the blender and blend until smooth.
2. Serve and enjoy.

Cal: 179kcal | Carb: 13.1g | Fat: 14.5g | Prot: 3g | Sugar: 3g | Cholesterol: 0mg

147. Choco Sunflower Butter Smoothie

 5 mins   5 mins

 10 mins   1

- ⅓ cup unsweetened coconut milk
- ¼ cup ice
- ½ tsp vanilla
- 1 tsp unsweetened cocoa powder
- ⅔ cup water
- 2 tbsp. sunflower seed butter

1. Add all ingredients into the blender and blend until smooth.
2. Serve and enjoy.

Cal: 379kcal | Carb: 13g | Fat: 34.6g | Prot: 8.5g | Sugar: 3g | Cholesterol: 0mg

148. Cinnamon Coconut Smoothie

 5 mins   5 mins

 10 mins   1

- ½ tsp cinnamon
- 1 scoop vanilla protein powder
- 1 tbsp. shredded coconut
- ¾ cup unsweetened almond milk
- ¼ cup unsweetened coconut milk

1. Add all ingredients into the blender and blend until smooth.
2. Serve and enjoy.

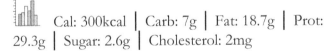 Cal: 300kcal | Carb: 7g | Fat: 18.7g | Prot: 29.3g | Sugar: 2.6g | Cholesterol: 2mg

149. Blackberry Smoothie

 5 mins   5 mins

 10 mins   2

- 1 cup unsweetened almond milk
- ½ cup ice
- ½ tsp vanilla
- 1 tsp erythritol
- 2 oz. (57 g) cream cheese, softened
- 4 tbsp. heavy whipping cream
- 2 oz. (57 g) fresh blackberries

1. Add all ingredients into the blender and blend until smooth.
2. Serve and enjoy.

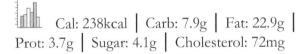 Cal: 238kcal | Carb: 7.9g | Fat: 22.9g | Prot: 3.7g | Sugar: 4.1g | Cholesterol: 72mg

150. Energy Booster Breakfast Smoothie

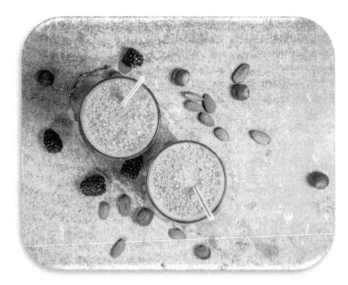

 5 mins   5 mins

 10 mins   1

- 1 cup unsweetened almond milk
- ½ cup ice
- 1 ½ tsp maca powder
- 1 tbsp. almond butter
- 1 tbsp. MCT oil

1. Add all ingredients into the blender and blend until smooth.
2. Serve and enjoy.

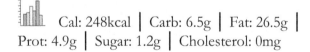 Cal: 248kcal | Carb: 6.5g | Fat: 26.5g | Prot: 4.9g | Sugar: 1.2g | Cholesterol: 0mg

151. Creamy Raspberry Smoothie

 5 mins   5 mins

 10 mins   2

- 1 cup unsweetened almond milk
- ½ tsp vanilla
- 1 tbsp. cream cheese, softened
- 2 tbsp. swerve
- ¼ cup fresh raspberries
- 4 tbsp. heavy cream
- 1 cup ice

1. Add all ingredients into the blender and blend until smooth and creamy.
2. Serve and enjoy.

Cal: 157kcal | Carb: 5.9g | Fat: 14.7g | Prot: 1.7g | Sugar: 0.9g | Cholesterol: 47mg

152. Coconut Avocado Smoothie

- 1 cup unsweetened coconut milk
- 1 tsp chia seeds
- 1 tsp lime juice
- 5 spinach leaves
- ½ avocado
- 1 tsp ginger

1. Add all ingredients into the blender and blend until smooth.
2. Serve and enjoy.

Cal: 104 kcal | Fat: 7.6 g | Carbs: 7.1 g | Sugar: 0.3 g | Prot: 2.6 g | Cholesterol: 0 m

 5 mins
 5 mins
 10 mins
 1

BONUS
FAST RECIPES

MEAT

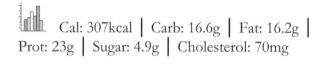 Cal: 307kcal | Carb: 16.6g | Fat: 16.2g | Prot: 23g | Sugar: 4.9g | Cholesterol: 70mg

153. Turkey Sandwich

 10 mins   5 mins

 15 mins   1

- 2 bread slices
- 3 oz. (85 g) turkey breast, cooked and shredded
- 1 tbsp. mayonnaise
- 1 cheese slice

1. Spread mayo on one side of each bread slice.
2. Take 1 bread slice and top with turkey and cheese.
3. Cover with the remaining bread slice.
4. Preheat the grill to high heat.
5. Spray the grill top with cooking spray.
6. Place the sandwich on the hot grill top and cook for 5 minutes or until golden brown from both sides.
7. Serve and enjoy.

154. Roast Beef Sandwich

 10 mins   5 mins

 15 mins   1

- 2 bread slices
- 2 cheese slices
- 4 deli roast beef, sliced
- 2 tsp. butter
- 1 tbsp. mayonnaise
- ¼ cup caramelized onions, sliced

1. Spread butter on one side of each bread slice.
2. Take 1 bread slice and spread with mayo top with beef, onion, and cheese.
3. Cover with the remaining bread slice.
4. Preheat the grill to high heat.
5. Spray the grill top with cooking spray.
6. Place the sandwich on the hot grill top and cook for 5 minutes or until golden brown from both sides.

7. Serve and enjoy.

 Cal: 859kcal │ Carb: 25.4g │ Fat: 44.6g │ Prot: 83.4g │ Sugar: 5.5g │ Cholesterol: 265mg

155. Asian Pork Skewers

10 mins   8 mins

18 mins   12

- 1 ½ lb. (230 g) pork tenderloin, cut into 1-inch (2,5 cm) pieces

For Marinade:
- ¾ tsp. cornstarch
- ¼ tsp. cayenne
- ½ tsp. pepper
- 2 tsp. Five-spice powder
- ½ cup hoisin sauce
- 1 ¼ tsp. salt

1. Add the pork pieces and the marinade ingredients into a mixing bowl and mix well and let it marinate for 30 minutes.
2. Preheat the grill to high heat.
3. Spray the grill top with cooking spray.
4. Thread the marinated pork pieces onto the skewers.

5. Place the skewers on the hot grill top and cook for 3–4 minutes on each side.
6. Serve and enjoy.

 Cal: 114kcal │ Carb: 5.5g │ Fat: 2.4g │ Prot: 15.8g │ Sugar: 2.9g │ Cholesterol: 42mg

FISH AND SEAFOOD

156. Coconut Pineapple Shrimp Skewers

20 mins   5 mins

25 mins   4

- 1–½ lb. (680 g) uncooked jumbo shrimp, peeled and deveined
- ½ cup light coconut milk
- 1 tbsp. cilantro, chopped
- 4 tsp. Tabasco Original Red Sauce
- 2 tsp. soy sauce
- ¼ cup freshly squeezed orange juice
- ¼ cup freshly squeezed lime juice (from about 2 large limes)
- ¾ lb. (340 g) pineapple, cut into 1-inch (2,5 cm) chunks
- Olive oil, for grilling

1. Combine the coconut milk, cilantro, Tabasco sauce, soy sauce, orange juice, and lime juice. Add the shrimp and toss to coat.
2. Cover and place in the refrigerator to marinate for 1 hour.
3. Thread the shrimp and pineapple onto metal skewers, alternating each.
4. Preheat grill to medium heat.
5. Add oil and cook for 5–6 minutes, flipping once, until the shrimp turn opaque pink.
6. Serve immediately.

Cal: 150kcal │ Carb: 14.9g │ Fat: 10.8g │ Prot: 1.5g │ Sodium: 190mg │ Dietary Fiber: 1.9g

157. **Spicy Grilled Squid**

 20 mins   5 mins

 25 mins   4

- 1 ½ lb. (230 g) Squid, prepared
- 2 tbps Olive oil

For the Marinade:

- 2 garlic cloves, minced
- ½ tsp. ginger, minced
- 3 tbsp. gochujang
- 3 tbsp. corn syrup
- 1 tsp. yellow mustard

- 1 tsp. soy sauce
- 2 tsp. sesame oil
- 1 tsp. sesame seeds
- 2 green onions, chopped

1. Preheat the grill to medium-high heat and brush with olive oil.
2. Add the squid and tentacles to the grill and cook for 1 minute until the bottom looks firm and opaque.
3. Turn them over and cook for another minute; straighten out the body with tongs if it curls.
4. Baste with sauce on top of the squid and cook for 2 additional minutes.
5. Flip and baste the other side, cook for 1 minute until the sauce evaporates and the squid turns red and shiny.

Cal: 292kcal │ Carb: 25.1g │ Fat: 8.6g │ Prot: 27.8g │ Sodium: 466mg │ Dietary Fiber: 2.7g

158. **Summer Shrimp Salad**

 20 mins   3 mins

 23 mins   5

- ½ pint cherry tomatoes
- 3 tbsp. olive oil

118

- ½ tsp. salt
- 1 lb. (450 g) medium to thin asparagus, woody stems snapped off and discarded
- 1 lb. (450 g) shelled and deveined medium shrimp
- ¼ tsp. freshly ground black pepper
- ¼ tsp. dried thyme
- Grated zest and juice of ½ lemon

Preparing the Ingredients:

1. Cut the cherry tomatoes into quarters and put them in a medium bowl. Add 1 tablespoon of olive oil and ¼ teaspoon of salt. Toss gently and set aside.
2. In a medium bowl, pour 1 tablespoon of the olive oil over the asparagus spears and rub gently to coat them.
3. Turn the control knob to the high position. Oil the grill and allow it to heat until the oil is shimmering but not smoking. Grill the asparagus for about 5 minutes. The thicker ones will still have a bit of crunch to them and the thinner ones will be tender. Transfer to a cutting board; keep the grill on high. When they are cool enough to handle, cut the spears into 1-inch (2,5 cm) pieces. Add to the cherry tomatoes.
4. Rinse the shrimp and pat dry with paper towels. Put them in a medium bowl, add the remaining tablespoon of olive oil, and toss to coat. Grill the shrimp for about 3 minutes, until they are opaque and firm to the touch.
5. Add the shrimp to the tomatoes and asparagus. Add the remaining ¼ tsp. salt, pepper, thyme, and lemon juice, and zest, and toss to combine. Serve warm or at room temperature, or refrigerate and serve chilled.

Cal: 240kcal | Carb: 5.8g | Fat: 13g | Prot: 25g

VEGETABLES

159. Grilled Zucchini

 5 mins   10 mins

 15 mins   6

- 4 medium zucchini
- 2 tbsp. olive oil
- 1 tbsp. sherry vinegar
- 2 sprigs thyme, leaves chopped
- ½ tsp. salt
- ⅓ tsp. ground black pepper

1. Switch on the gas grill, fill the grill hopper with oak flavored grill, power the grill on by using the control panel, select 'smoke' on the temperature dial, or set the temperature to 350 °F (180 °C) and let it preheat for a minimum of 5 minutes.
2. Meanwhile, cut the ends of each zucchini, cut each in half and then into thirds, and place in a plastic bag.
3. Add the remaining ingredients, seal the bag, and shake well to coat the zucchini pieces.
4. When the grill has preheated, open the lid, place the zucchini on the grill grate, shut the grill, and smoke for 4 minutes per side.

5. When done, transfer the zucchini to a dish, garnish with more thyme and then serve.

 Cal: 74kcal | Carb: 6.1g | Fat: 5.4g | Prot: 2.6g | Fiber: 2.3g

160. Southern Slaw

 10 mins   0 min

 10 mins   4

- 1 head cabbage, shredded
- ¼ cup white vinegar
- ¼ cup sugar
- 1 tsp. paprika
- ½ tsp. salt
- ½ tsp. freshly ground black pepper
- 1 cup heavy (whipping) cream

1. Place the shredded cabbage in a large bowl.
2. In a small bowl, combine the vinegar, sugar, paprika, salt, and pepper.
3. Pour the vinegar mixture over the cabbage and mix well.
4. Fold in the heavy cream and refrigerate for at least 1 hour before serving.

 Cal: 130kcal | Carb: 5g | Fat: -22.9g | Prot: 79g | Sodium: 45mg | Cholesterol: 19mg

161. Grilled Vegetables

 5 mins   15 mins

 20 mins   8

- 1 veggie tray
- ¼ cup vegetable oil
- 2 tbsp. veggie seasoning

1. Preheat the grill to 375 °F (190 °C) .
2. Toss the vegetables in oil and then place them on a sheet pan.
3. Sprinkle with veggie seasoning then place them on the hot grill.
4. Grill for 15 minutes or until the veggies are cooked.
5. Let rest then serve. Enjoy.

 Cal: 44kcal | Carb: 1g | Fat: 5g | Prot: -1.3g | Saturated Fat: 0g | Sodium: 36mg | Potassium: 10mg

GRILL BREAD

162. Garlic Parmesan Grill Cheese Sandwiches

 2 mins   7 mins

 9 mins   1

- 2 slices Italian bread, sliced thin
- 2 slices provolone cheese
- 2 tbsp. butter, softened
- Garlic powder, for dusting
- Dried parsley, for dusting
- Parmesan cheese, shredded, for dusting

1. Spread butter evenly across 2 slices of bread and sprinkle each buttered side with garlic and parsley.
2. Sprinkle a few tablespoons of Parmesan cheese over each buttered side of bread and gently press the cheese into the bread.
3. Preheat the grill to medium heat and place one slice of bread, buttered side down, into the grill.
4. Top with provolone slices and the second slice of bread with the butter side up.
5. Cook for 3 minutes, and flip to cook for 3 minutes on the other side; cook until the bread is golden and the Parmesan cheese is crispy.
6. Serve warm with your favorite sides!

Cal: 575kcal | Carb: 18.1g | Fat: 45.1g | Prot: 27.6g | Sodium: 1065mg | Dietary Fiber: 2.8g

163. Sun-Dried Tomato and Chicken Flatbreads

 5 mins   7 mins

 12 mins   4

- Flatbreads or thin pita bread

For the Topping:
- ½ cup sliced Grill chicken, pre-cooked or leftovers
- ½ cup sun-dried tomatoes, coarsely chopped
- 3 leaves fresh basil, coarsely chopped
- 2 cups mozzarella cheese, shredded
- 1 tsp. salt
- 1 tsp. ground black pepper
- 1 tsp. red pepper flakes
- Olive or chili oil, for serving

1. Preheat the grill to low heat.

2. Mix all the topping ingredients together in a large mixing bowl with a rubber spatula.
3. Lay flatbreads on the grill, and top with an even amount of topping mixture; spreading to the edges of each.
4. Tent the flatbreads with foil for 5 minutes each, or until the cheese is just melted.
5. Place the flatbreads on a flat surface or cutting board and cut each with a pizza cutter or kitchen scissors.
6. Drizzle with olive or chili oil to serve!

Cal: 276kcal | Carb: 35.7g | Fat: 5.7g | Prot: 19.8g | Sodium: 1061mg | Dietary Fiber: 1.9g

1. Preheat the grill to medium heat.
2. Brush the bread slices with oil and place them on the hot grill top and cook until lightly golden brown from both sides.
3. In a bowl, add all the topping ingredients and mix well.
4. Spoon the topping mixture over the bread slices.
5. Serve and enjoy.

Cal: 304kcal | Carb: 36.7g | Fat: 13.3g | Prot: 9g | Sugar: 2.5g | Cholesterol: 8mg

164. <u>Artichoke Bruschetta</u>

SNACKS & HANDS DISHES

165. <u>Tortilla Pizza</u>

 10 mins   5 mins

 15 mins   4

- 8 oz. (230 g) baguette bread, cut into 1-inch (2,5 cm) slices
- 2 tbsp. olive oil

For Topping:
- 1 cup can artichokes, drained and chopped
- 2 cups baby spinach, chopped
- ¼ cup mayonnaise
- ¼ cup Parmesan cheese, grated
- ½ tsp. salt

 10 mins   5 mins

 15 mins   1

- 1 tortilla

For Topping:
- ¼ tsp. red chili flakes
- ¼ tsp. dried oregano
- ½ tsp. garlic, minced
- 2 tsp. onion, chopped

- ¼ cup tomatoes, chopped
- 3 tbsp. mozzarella cheese, shredded
- Salt and pepper to taste

1. Add tomatoes, onion, garlic, oregano, chili flakes, cheese, pepper, and salt to a tortilla.
2. Preheat the grill to high heat.
3. Spray the grill top with cooking spray.
4. Place the tortilla on the hot grill top, cover, and cook until the cheese melts.
5. Serve and enjoy.

Cal: 336kcal | Carb: 18g | Fat: 15.8g | Prot: 26.1g | Sugar: 1.4g | Cholesterol: 45mg

166. **Chicken Pizza Sandwich**

 10 mins   5 mins

 15 mins   2

- 4 bread slices
- 1 chicken breast, cooked and sliced
- 1 tbsp. butter
- 4 mozzarella cheese slices
- 2 tbsp. olives, sliced
- 2 tbsp. pizza sauce
- 8 pepperoni slices

1. Spread butter on one side of each bread slice.
2. Take 2 bread slices and spread with pizza sauce and top with chicken, pepperoni slices, olives, and cheese.
3. Cover with remaining bread slices.
4. Preheat the grill to high heat.
5. Spray grill top with cooking spray.
6. Place sandwiches on a hot grill top and cook for 5 minutes or until lightly golden brown from both sides.
7. Servings and enjoy.

Cal: 443kcal | Carb: 13.4g | Fat: 28.3g | Prot: 33.4g | Sugar: 1.3g | Cholesterol: 100mg

167. **Healthy Broccoli**

 10 mins   6 mins

 16 mins   6

- 4 cups broccoli florets
- 1 ½ tsp garlic, minced
- 1 ½ tsp Italian seasoning
- 1 tbsp. lemon juice
- 4 tbsp. olive oil
- ¼ tsp pepper
- 1 ¼ tsp salt

1. Add broccoli and remaining ingredients into the bowl and mix well. Cover and place in the refrigerator for 1 hour.
2. Preheat the grill to high heat.
3. Spray grill top with cooking spray.
4. Place broccoli florets on a hot grill top and cook for 3 minutes on each side.
5. Servings and enjoy.

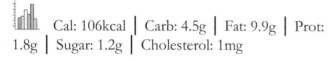 Cal: 106kcal │ Carb: 4.5g │ Fat: 9.9g │ Prot: 1.8g │ Sugar: 1.2g │ Cholesterol: 1mg

MARINADES, SAUCES

168. Lemon and Thyme Sauce

 4 mins   0 min

 4 mins   2 cups

- 1 cup low-sodium chicken broth
- ½ cup freshly squeezed lemon juice
- ¼ cup cooking oil
- ¼ cup water
- 1 tablespoon finely minced fresh chives
- 1 tablespoon fresh thyme
- 1 tablespoon finely minced garlic

1. Put ingredients in a medium bowl and whisk until combined. Use immediately or store refrigerated for up to 10 days.

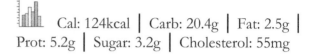 Cal: 124kcal │ Carb: 20.4g │ Fat: 2.5g │ Prot: 5.2g │ Sugar: 3.2g │ Cholesterol: 55mg

169. White Wine Sherry Sauce

 4 mins   0 min

 4 mins   2 cups

- 1 cup dry white wine
- ½ cup water
- ¼ cup cooking sherry
- ¼ cup cooking oil
- 2 tablespoons finely minced shallots
- 1 tablespoon dried parsley
- 1 tablespoon finely minced garlic
- 1 tablespoon finely minced capers
- 1 teaspoon salt
- 1 teaspoon pepper

1. Put ingredients in a medium bowl and whisk until combined. Use immediately or store refrigerated for up to 10 days.

Cal: 243kcal | Carb: 25.7g | Fat: 1.6g |
Prot: 31.4g | Sugar: 17.3g | Cholesterol: 59mg

170. Ketchup Juice Sauce

 4 mins   0 min

 4 mins   2 cups

- 1 cup ketchup
- ⅓ cup cider vinegar
- ⅓ cup apple juice
- ¼ cup Worcestershire sauce
- ¼ cup sriracha
- 2 tablespoons water
- 2 tablespoons onion powder
- 2 tablespoons garlic powder
- 2 tablespoons sugar
- 2 tablespoons brown sugar
- 2 tablespoons tomato paste

1. Put ingredients in a medium bowl and whisk until combined. Use immediately or store refrigerated for up to 10 days.

 Cal: 208kcal | Carb: 18.9g | Fat: 13.3g |
Prot: 3.9g | Sugar: 0.8g | Cholesterol: 0mg

SWEET RECIPES

171. Seasonal Fruit on the Grill

 5 mins   10 mins

 15 mins   4

- 2 plums, peaches apricots, etc. (choose seasonally)
- 3 tablespoons Sugar, turbinate
- ¼ cup of Honey
- Gelato, as desired

1. Preheat the grill to 450F with closed lid.
2. Slice each fruit in halves and remove pits. Brush with honey. Sprinkle with some sugar.
3. Grill on the grate until you see that there are grill marks. Set aside.
4. Serve each with a scoop of gelato. Enjoy.

Cal: 120kcal | Carb: 15g | Fat: 3g | Prot: 1g

172. <u>Juicy Loosey Smokey Burger</u>

 30 mins 30 mins

 1 h 2

- 1-pound (450 g) Beef
- ⅓ pound (150 g) per burger
- Cheddar cheese
- Grill AP Rub
- Salt
- Freshly Ground Black Pepper
- Hamburger Bun
- BBQ Sauce

1. Split every ⅓ pound (150 g) of meat, which is 2.66 ounces (75 g) per half.
2. Level out one half to roughly 6 inches (15,2 cm) plate. Put wrecked of American cheddar, leaving ½ inch (1,3 cm) clear.
3. Put another portion of the meat on top, and seal edges. Rehash for all burgers.
4. Sprinkle with Grill AP rub, salt, and pepper flame broil seasonings.
5. Smoke at 250 for 50mins. No compelling reason to turn.
6. Apply Smokey Dokey BBQ sauce, ideally a mustard-based sauce like Grill Gold and Bold, or Sticky Fingers Carolina Classic.

Cook for an extra 10 minutes, or to favored doneness.

 Cal: 264kcal | Carb: 57g | Fat: 2g | Prot: 4g

SIDES AND SALADS

173. <u>Watermelon-Cucumber Salad</u>

 12 mins 0 min

 12 mins 4

- 1 tablespoon olive oil
- 2 teaspoons fresh lemon juice
- ¼ teaspoon salt
- 2 cups cubed seedless watermelon
- 1 cup thinly sliced English cucumber
- ¼ cup thinly vertically sliced red onion
- 1 tablespoon thinly sliced fresh basil

1. Consolidate oil, juice, and salt in a huge bowl, mixing great. Include watermelon, cucumber, and onion; toss well to coat. Sprinkle plate of mixed greens equally with basil.

Cal: 60kcal | Carb: 7.6g | Fat: 3.5g | Prot: 0.8g

174. Tequila Slaw with Lime and Cilantro

175. Banana Cinnamon Coconut Fritters

 5 mins   4 mins

 9 mins   12 fritters

 5 mins   5 mins

 10 mins   6

- 2 bananas, mashed
- ⅓ cup flour
- ½ tsp. cinnamon
- 2 eggs
- ½ cup shredded coconut

- ¼ cup canola mayonnaise (such as Hellmann's)
- 3 tablespoons fresh lime juice
- 1 tablespoon silver tequila
- 2 teaspoons sugar
- ¼ teaspoon salt
- ⅓ cup thinly sliced green onions
- ¼ cup chopped fresh cilantro
- 1 (14-ounce (400 g)) package coleslaw

1. Combine all fixings except oil in a bowl— Preheat grill pan for 4 minutes on medium heat. Coat the pan with canola oil. Drop heaping tablespoons of fritter batter onto the pan. Serve.

 Cal: 115kcal | Carb: 11g | Fat: 7g | Prot: 2g

1. Add the first 5 ingredients to a big bowl. Add remaining ingredients; toss.

 Cal: 64kcal | Carb: 6.4g | Fat: 3g | Prot: 0.8g

176. <u>Grilled Pineapple Disk with Vanilla Bean Ice Cream</u>

 5 mins 4 mins

 9 mins 4

- 1 whole pineapple, sliced into 6 equal slices
- 6 scoops of vanilla bean ice cream
- 6 spoonsful of whipped cream
- ¼ cup almond slivers, toasted
- ¼ cup sweetened shredded coconut, toasted
- ½ cup caramel sauce
- Mint (to garnish)

1.	Bring the gas grill to medium-low heat. Oil your grill and allow it to heat until the oil is shimmering but not smoking. Grill pineapple until a nice char forms, about 2 minutes per side.
2.	Remove pineapple from the grill, top each slice with a scoop of ice cream, a dollop of whipped cream, almonds, and coconut. Drizzle each with caramel sauce, garnish with mint, and serve.

 Cal: 140kcal | Carb: 19g | Fat: 6g | Prot: 2g

177. <u>Buttered Popcorn</u>

 5 mins 4 mins

 9 mins 2-4

- 3 tablespoons peanut oil
- ½ cup popcorn kernels
- 3 tablespoons butter
- Salt, to taste

1.	Prepare your grill for two-zone cooking. Set the gas grill to medium-high heat and add the peanut oil. While it is heating, place 5 popcorn kernels in the oil.
2.	When 2 or 3 pop, add the butter to the oil and pour in the remaining kernels. Cover immediately with a tall pan or spaghetti pot.
3.	When the popcorn starts popping, you will need to stir it in the oil to get all the kernels to pop and prevent the popped corn from burning.
4.	Using insulated gloves, potholders, or thick kitchen towels, agitate the popcorn by moving the pan or pot from side to side on the grill without lifting.
5.	Cook within 4 minutes, or until the popping slows down to once every few seconds. When all the corn is popped, slide the pot or pan and popcorn to the cool side of the grill and remove the lid.
6.	Use two spatulas to scoop up the hot popcorn and transfer it to a bowl. Serve with salt and additional seasonings as desired.

 Cal: 170kcal | Carb: 13g | Fat: 12g | Prot: 2g

BONUS
GLUTEN FREE RECIPES

MEAT

178. Greek Pork Skewers

 10 mins

 10 mins

 20 mins

 8

- 2 lb. (910 g) pork tenderloin, cut into cubes
- 1 onion, cut into chunks
- 2 bell pepper, cut into chunks

For Marinade:
- ½ tsp. ground coriander
- 1 tsp. ground cumin
- 2 tbsp. parsley, chopped
- 1 tbsp. garlic, chopped
- ½ cup olive oil
- ½ cup vinegar
- ¼ tsp. pepper
- ½ tsp. salt

1. Add the pork cubes and the marinade ingredients into a zip-lock bag and mix well.

The sealed bag is shaken well and placed in the refrigerator for 8 hours.
2. Thread the marinated pork cubes, bell pepper, and onion onto the skewers.
3. Preheat the grill to high heat.
4. Spray the grill top with cooking spray.
5. Place the skewers on the hot grill top and cook for 10 minutes or until the internal temperature of pork cubes reaches 145 °F (60 °C) . Turn the skewers 2–3 times.
6. Serve and enjoy.

Cal: 288kcal | Carb: 3.4g | Fat: 16.7g | Prot: 30.3g | Sugar: 1.4g | Cholesterol: 83mg

179. Honey Soy Pork Chops

 10 mins

 10 mins

 20 mins

 6

- 6 pork chops, boneless
- 1 tbsp. vinegar

- 2 tbsp. olive oil
- 1 tbsp. soy sauce
- ¼ cup honey
- Salt and pepper to taste

1. Add the pork chops and the remaining ingredients into a zip-lock bag and mix well. The sealed bag is shaken well and placed in the refrigerator for 2 hours.
2. Preheat the grill to medium heat.
3. Spray the grill top with cooking spray.
4. Place the pork chops on the hot grill top and cook for 5 minutes on each side or until the internal temperature reaches 145 °F (60 °C) .
5. Serve and enjoy.

Cal: 341kcal | Carb: 11.9g | Fat: 24.6g | Prot: 18.2g | Sugar: 11.7g | Cholesterol: 69mg

180. Pineapple Honey Pork Chops

 10 mins   12 mins

 22 mins   4

- 4 pork chops, boneless
- 1 tbsp. Dijon mustard

- ¼ cup honey
- 8 oz. (230 g) crushed pineapple
- Salt and pepper to taste

1. Add the pork chops and the remaining ingredients into a zip-lock bag. Seal the bag, shake well, and place it in the refrigerator overnight.
2. Preheat the grill to high heat.
3. Spray the grill top with cooking spray.
4. Place the pork chops on the hot grill top and cook for 5–6 minutes on each side.
5. Serve and enjoy.

Cal: 351kcal | Carb: 25.1g | Fat: 20.1g | Prot: 18.5g | Sugar: 23g | Cholesterol: 69mg

181. Lamb Skewers

 10 mins   12 mins

 22 mins   4

- 1 ½ lb. (230 g) leg of lamb, cut into 1-inch (2,5 cm) pieces

For Marinade:
- 1 tsp. ground cumin
- 1 ½ tsp. paprika
- ¾ cup olive oil

- 1 tsp. red pepper flakes
- 1 tbsp. vinegar
- 1 tbsp. lemon juice
- 2 tbsp. shallot
- ¼ cup chives
- ¼ cup parsley
- ¼ cup mint
- Salt to taste

1. Add all marinade ingredients into a blender and blend until smooth.
2. Pour the blended mixture into a mixing bowl. Add lamb pieces and mix well and let it marinate for 2 hours.
3. Thread the marinated lamb pieces onto the skewers.
4. Preheat the grill to high heat.
5. Spray the grill top with cooking spray.
6. Place the skewers on the hot grill top and cook for 6 minutes or until the lamb is cooked.
7. Serve and enjoy.

Cal: 656kcal | Carb: 2.7g | Fat: 50.7g | Prot: 48.6g | Sugar: 0.3g | Cholesterol: 153mg

182. Healthy Lamb Patties

 10 mins   10 mins

 20 mins   4

- 1 egg
- 1 lb. (450 g) ground lamb meat
- ½ tbsp. garlic, minced
- ½ tbsp. chili powder
- Salt and pepper to taste

2. Add all ingredients into a bowl and mix until well combined.
3. Preheat the grill to high heat.
4. Spray the grill top with cooking spray.

Make patties from the mixture and place them on the hot grill top and cook for 5 minutes on each side.

FISH AND SEAFOOD

183. Parmesan Shrimp

 20 mins   6 mins

 26 mins   4

- 1 lb. (450 g) shrimp, peeled and deveined
- 2 tbsp. Parmesan cheese, grated
- 1 tbsp. fresh lemon juice
- 1 tbsp. pine nuts, toasted
- 1 garlic clove

131

- ½ cup basil
- 1 tbsp. olive oil
- Salt and pepper to taste

1. Add basil, lemon juice, cheese, pine nuts, garlic, pepper, and salt in a blender and blend until smooth.
2. Add the shrimp and basil paste to a bowl and mix well.
3. Place the shrimp bowl in the fridge for 20 minutes.
4. Preheat the grill to high heat.
5. Spray the grill top with cooking spray.
6. Thread the marinated shrimp onto skewers and place the skewers on the hot grill top.
7. Cook the shrimp for 3 minutes on each side or until cooked.
8. Serve and enjoy.

Cal: 225kcal │ Carb: 2.2g │ Fat: 11.2g │ Prot: 27.2g │ Sugar: 0.2g │ Cholesterol: 241mg

184. Halibut

 20 mins   7 mins

 27 mins   4

- 4 Halibut fillets, cut about 1 inch (2,5 cm) thick

- 2 tbsp Olive oil
- Sea salt and pepper to taste
- Fresh grated Parmesan cheese for topping
- Fresh chopped parsley for topping
- Fresh lemon juice for serving

1. Brush the halibut fillets with olive oil and sprinkle with salt and pepper.
2. Preheat the gas grill to high.
3. Spray the grill with spray oil and immediately place the halibut on the heat.
4. Grill for 2 minutes per side.
5. Turn the grill down to medium and grill for 2 minutes per side.
6. Sprinkle the halibut with the Parmesan and grill an additional minute before removing from the heat.
7. Sprinkle the fillets with parsley and lemon juice, and let them relax for 5 minutes before serving.

Cal: 223kcal │ Carb: 10g │ Fat: 5g │ Prot: 42g

185. Lobster Tails with Lime Basil Butter

 20 mins   6 mins

 26 mins   4

- 4 lobster tails (cut in half lengthwise)
- 3 tbsp. olive oil
- Lime wedges (to serve)
- Sea salt, to taste

For the Lime Basil Butter:
- 1 stick unsalted butter, softened
- ½ bunch basil, roughly chopped
- 1 lime, zested and juiced
- 2 garlic cloves, minced
- ¼ tsp. red pepper flakes

1. Add the butter ingredients to a mixing bowl and combine; set aside until ready to use.
2. Preheat grill to medium-high heat.
3. Drizzle the lobster tail halves with olive oil and season with salt and pepper.
4. Place the lobster tails, flesh-side down, on the grill.
5. Allow to cook until opaque, about 3 minutes, flip and cook another 3 minutes.
6. Add a dollop of the lime basil butter during the last minute of cooking.
7. Serve immediately with lemon wedges.

Cal: 430kcal | Carb: 2.4g | Fat: 34.7g | Prot: 28g | Sodium: 926mg | Dietary Fiber: 0.5g

 20 mins   10 mins

 30 mins   2

- ½ lb. (230 g) shrimp, peeled and deveined
- 1 tbsp. garlic, minced
- ⅓ cup olives
- 1 cup mushrooms, sliced
- 2 tbsp. olive oil
- 1 cup tomatoes, diced
- 1 small onion, chopped
- Salt and pepper to taste

1. Preheat the grill to high heat. Add oil.
2. Add onion, mushrooms, and garlic and sauté until the onion softens.
3. Add the shrimp and tomatoes and stir until the shrimp is cooked through.
4. Add olives and stir well.
5. Remove the pan from heat and set aside for 5 minutes. Season with pepper and salt.
6. Serve and enjoy.

Cal: 325kcal | Carb: 12.5g | Fat: 18.7g | Prot: 28.6g | Sugar: 4.5g | Cholesterol: 239mg

186. **Shrimp Veggie Stir Fry**

VEGETABLES

187. Sweet Onion Bake

 10 mins   45 mins

 55 mins   4

- 4 large Vidalia or other sweet onions
- 8 tbsp. (1 stick) unsalted butter, melted

188. Roasted Okra

 10 mins   30 mins

- 4 chicken bouillon cubes
- 1 cup grated Parmesan cheese

1. Preheat the grill to 350 °F (180 °C) .
2. Coat a high-sided baking pan with cooking spray or butter.
3. Peel the onions and cut them into quarters, separating them into individual petals.
4. Spread the onions out in the prepared pan and pour the melted butter over them.
5. Crush the bouillon cubes and sprinkle over the buttery onion pieces, and then top with the cheese.
6. Transfer the pan to the grill, close the lid, and smoke for 30 minutes.
7. Remove the pan from the grill, cover tightly with aluminum foil, and poke several holes all over to vent.
8. Place the pan back on the grill, close the lid, and smoke for an additional 30 to 45 minutes.
9. Uncover the onions, stir, and serve hot.

 Cal: 50kcal | Carb: 4g | Fat: 2.5g | Prot: 2g | Fiber: 2g

 40 mins   4

- 1 lb. (450 g) whole okra
- 2 tbsp. extra-virgin olive oil
- 2 tsp. seasoned salt
- 2 tsp. freshly ground black pepper

1. Preheat the grill to 400 °F (200 °C) .
2. Line a shallow rimmed baking pan with aluminum foil and coat with cooking spray.
3. Arrange the okra on the pan in a single layer. Drizzle with the olive oil, turning to coat. Season on all sides with salt and pepper.
4. Place the baking pan on the grill grate, close the lid, and smoke for 30 minutes, or until crisp and slightly charred. Alternatively, roast in the oven for 30 minutes.

5. Serve hot.

 Cal: 150kcal | Carb: 15g | Fat: -25.1g | Prot: 79g | Sodium: 45mg | Cholesterol: 49mg

189. **Sweet Potato Chips**

 10 mins   45 mins

 55 mins   4

- 2 sweet potatoes
- 1 quart warm water
- 1 tbsp. cornstarch, plus 2 tsp.
- ¼ cup extra-virgin olive oil
- 1 tbsp. salt
- 1 tbsp. packed brown sugar
- 1 tsp. ground cinnamon
- 1 tsp. freshly ground black pepper
- ½ tsp. cayenne pepper

1. Using a mandolin, thinly slice the sweet potatoes.
2. Pour the warm water into a large bowl and add 1 tablespoon of cornstarch and the potato slices. Let soak for 15 to 20 minutes.
3. Preheat the grill to 375 °F (190 °C) .
4. Drain the potato slices, then arrange in a single layer on a perforated pizza pan or a baking sheet lined with aluminum foil. Brush the potato slices on both sides with olive oil.
5. In a small bowl, whisk together the salt, brown sugar, cinnamon, black pepper, cayenne pepper, and the remaining 2 teaspoons of cornstarch. Sprinkle this seasoning blend on both sides of the potatoes.
6. Place the pan or baking sheet on the grill grate, close the lid, and smoke for 35 to 45 minutes, flipping after 20 minutes until the chips curl up and become crispy.
7. Store in an airtight container.

Ingredient Tip: Avoid storing your sweet potatoes in the refrigerator's produce bin, which tends to give them a hard center and an unpleasant flavor. What, you don't have a root cellar? Just keep them in a cool, dry area of your kitchen.

 Cal: 150kcal | Carb: 15g | Fat: -25.1g | Prot: 79g | Sodium: 45mg | Cholesterol: 49mg

GRILL BREAD

190. **Cheesesteak**

 10 mins   8 mins

 18 mins   6

- 2 lb. (910 g) ground beef

- 6 buns
- ¾ cup white onion, chopped
- 2 slices yellow American cheese
- 1 tsp. garlic powder
- ½ tsp. onion powder
- ½ tsp. pepper
- ½ tsp. salt

1. Preheat the grill to high heat.
2. Add white onion and cook for 5 minutes
3. Add the beef and chop it
4. Season with salt, pepper, garlic, and onion powder
5. Separately, toast the buns for 20 seconds
6. Add cheese to the beef. Spray water and cover it for a few minutes.
7. Remove from the grill, place on the buns, and enjoy.

Cal: 292kcal | Carb: 2.5g | Fat: 9.4g | Prot: 46.1g | Sugar: 1.6g | Cholesterol: 135mg

SNACKS & HANDS DISHES

191. Scallops Orange Skewers

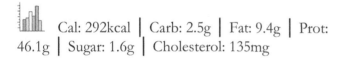

 10 mins   10 mins

 20 mins   2

- 12 scallops
- 1 tbsp. ginger, grated
- 1 orange, cut into pieces
- 1 tbsp. honey
- Salt and pepper to taste

1. In a small bowl, mix honey, ginger, pepper, and salt.
2. Thread the scallops and orange pieces onto the skewers and brush with the honey mixture.
3. Preheat the grill to medium heat.
4. Place the skewers on the hot grill top and cook for 2–3 minutes on each side.
5. Serve and enjoy.

Cal: 243kcal | Carb: 25.7g | Fat: 1.6g | Prot: 31.4g | Sugar: 17.3g | Cholesterol: 59mg

192. Chickpea Burger Patties

 10 mins   12 mins

 22 mins   6

- 3 eggs
- 1 ¾ cups can chickpeas, drained

- 2 cups cauliflower florets
- ½ tsp. onion powder
- 1 tsp. garlic powder
- 2 tbsp. parsley, chopped
- ½ cup onion, chopped
- Salt and pepper to taste

1. Add cauliflower florets and chickpeas into a food processor and process until finely chopped.
2. Add the remaining ingredients and process until just combined.
3. Preheat the grill to medium heat.
4. Make patties from the mixture and place them on the hot grill top and cook until lightly browned from both sides.
5. Serve and enjoy.

 Cal: 130kcal | Carb: 19.3g | Fat: 3g | Prot: 7.2g | Sugar: 1.6g | Cholesterol: 82mg

MARINADES, SAUCES

193. Vinegar Honey Sauce

 4 mins

 0 min

 4 mins

 2 cups

- 1¼ cups balsamic vinegar
- ½ cup water
- ¼ cup honey
- ¼ cup cooking oil
- 1 tablespoon Italian seasoning
- 1 teaspoon salt
- 1 teaspoon white pepper

1. Put ingredients in a medium bowl and whisk until combined. Use immediately or store refrigerated for up to 10 days.

 Cal: 71kcal | Carb: 11g | Fat: 2.3g | Prot: 2.6g | Sugar: 3.2g | Cholesterol: 2mg

SWEET RECIPES

194. Apple Pie on the Grill

 15 mins

 30 mins

 45 mins

 6

- ¼ cup of Sugar
- 4 Apples, sliced
- 1 tablespoon of Cornstarch

- 1 teaspoon Cinnamon, ground
- 1 Pie Crust, refrigerated, soften in according to the directions on the box
- ½ cup of Peach preserves

1. Preheat the grill to 375F with closed lid.
2. In a bowl combine the cinnamon, cornstarch, sugar, and apples. Set aside.
3. Place the piecrust in a pie pan. Spread the preserves and then place the apples. Fold the crust slightly.
4. Place a pan on the grill (upside - down) so that you don't brill/bake the pie directly on the heat.
5. Cook 30 - 40 minutes. Once done, set aside to rest. Serve and enjoy

 Cal: 160kcal | Carb: 35g | Fat: 1g | Prot: 0.5g

195. <u>Caramel Bananas</u>

 15 mins   15 mins

 30 mins   4

- ⅓ cup chopped pecans
- ½ cup sweetened condensed milk
- 4 slightly green bananas
- ½ cup brown sugar

- 2 tablespoons corn syrup
- ½ cup butter

1. Preheat your grill, with the lid closed, until it reaches 350.
2. Place the milk, corn syrup, butter, and brown sugar into a heavy saucepan and bring to boil. For five minutes simmer the mixture in low heat. Stir frequently.
3. Place the bananas with their peels on, on the grill and let them grill for five minutes. Flip and cook for five minutes more. Peels will be dark and might split.
4. Place on serving platter. Cut the ends off the bananas and split peel down the middle. Take the peel off the bananas and spoon caramel on top. Sprinkle with pecans.

 Cal: 152kcal | Carb: 36g | Fat: 1g | Prot: 1g

<u>SIDES AND SALADS</u>

196. <u>Spinach Salad with Avocado and Orange</u>

 5 mins   20 mins

 25 mins   4

138

- 1 ½ tablespoon fresh lime juice
- 4 teaspoons extra-virgin olive oil
- 1 tablespoon chopped fresh cilantro
- 1/8 teaspoon salt
- ½ cup diced peeled ripe avocado
- ½ cup fresh orange segments
- 1 (5-ounce (140 g)) package baby spinach
- 1/8 teaspoon freshly ground black pepper

1. Combine the first 4 substances in a bowl, stirring with a whisk.
2. Combine avocado, orange segments, and spinach in a bowl. Add oil combination; toss. Sprinkle salad with black pepper.

 Cal: 103kcal | Fat: 7.3g | Sodium: 118mg

197. <u>Raspberry and Blue Cheese Salad</u>

 5 mins   20 mins

 25 mins   4

- 1 ½ tablespoon olive oil
- 1 ½ teaspoon red wine vinegar
- ¼ teaspoon Dijon mustard

- 1/8 teaspoon salt
- 1/8 teaspoon pepper
- 5 cups mixed baby greens
- ½ cup raspberries
- ¼ cup chopped toasted pecans
- 1-ounce (28 g) blue cheese

1. Join olive oil, vinegar, Dijon mustard, salt, and pepper.
2. Include blended baby greens, too.
3. Top with raspberries, pecans, and blue cheese.

 Cal: 133kcal | Fat: 12.2g | Sodium: 193mg

GRILL DESSERTS

198. <u>Honey Grilled Peaches</u>

 5 mins   5 mins

 10 mins   4

- Fresh peaches, as desired
- ½ Fresh honey, as desired
- Cinnamon to taste
- Coconut oil, as needed
- Plain yogurt or ice cream for topping

1. Slice the peaches lengthwise top to bottom and remove the pits. Drizzle honey on the cut side of the peach and sprinkle with cinnamon.
2. Bring the gas grill to medium-low heat. Oil the Grill and allow it to heat until the oil is shimmering but not smoking.
1. 3.Set the peaches sliced-side up and grill peaches for a couple of minutes cut side down, then flip and brush with coconut oil honey, and cinnamon
3. Grill for several minutes until the skin is starting to brown and pull back. Serve with vanilla ice cream while still warm.

 Cal: 132kcal | Carb: 32g | Fat: 0g | Prot: 13g

199. Rosemary Watermelon Steaks

 5 mins   10 mins

 15 mins   4-8

- 1 small watermelon, removed seeds
- ¼ cup good-quality olive oil
- 1 tablespoon minced fresh rosemary
- Salt and pepper, as needed
- Lemon wedges for serving

1. Heat a grill for medium heat. Cut the watermelon into 2-inch (5,1 cm) -thick slices, with the rind intact, and then into halves or quarters, if you like.
2. Place the oil and rosemary in a small bowl, sprinkle with salt and pepper, and stir. Brush or rub this batter all over the watermelon slices.
3. Place the watermelon on the grill directly. Cook turning once until the flesh develops grill marks and has dried out a bit, 4 to 5 minutes per side. Transfer it to your platter and serve with lemon wedges.

 Cal: 101kcal | Carb: 11g | Fat: 0g | Prot: 2g

BONUS
MEAL PLAN

MEAL PLAN WEEK 1

DAY	BREAKFAST	LUNCH	DINNER
MONDAY	Baked Asparagus Pancetta Cheese Tart	Smoked Mushrooms	Marinated Pork Chops
TUESDAY	Grill Fruit with Cream	Whole Roasted Cauliflower with Garlic Parmesan Butter	Parmesan Shrimp
WEDNESDAY	Bread Pudding	Grilled Vegetables	Easy Sirloin Steaks
THURSDAY	Sweet Potato Chips	Smoked Asparagus	Halibut
FRIDAY		Smoked Acorn Squash	Steak Sandwich
SATURDAY	Cold Smoked Cheese	Vegan Smoked Carrot Dogs	Greek Salmon Fillets
SUNDAY	Bacon Sweet Potato Pie	Smoked Vegetables	Pineapple Beef Burger Patties

MEAL PLAN WEEK 2

DAY	BREAKFAST	LUNCH	DINNER
MONDAY	Grill Spicy Sweet Potatoes	Grilled Stuffed Zucchini	Roast Beef Sandwich
TUESDAY	Apple Pie on the Grill	Green Beans with Bacon	Coconut Pineapple Shrimp Skewers
WEDNESDAY	Grilled Sugar Snap Peas	Grilled Potato Salad	Lemon Rosemary Cornish Hen
THURSDAY	Bacon-Wrapped Jalapeno Poppers	Vegetable Sandwich	Healthy Salmon Patties
FRIDAY	Grill Layered Cake	Cauliflower with Parmesan and Butter	Moroccan Chicken
SATURDAY	Quick Cheese Toast	Grilled Mexican Street Corn	Swordfish
SUNDAY	Smoked Chocolate Bacon Pecan Pie	Sweet Onion Bake	Asian Pork Skewers

MEAL PLAN WEEK 3

DAY	BREAKFAST	LUNCH	DINNER
MONDAY	Coconut Chocolate Simple Brownies	Grilled Zucchini	Classic Burger Patties
TUESDAY	Apple Cobbler	Grill Vegetable Pizza	Italian Shrimp
WEDNESDAY	Bacon Jalapeno Wraps	Ultimate Grill Cheese	Tomato Roast Beef Sandwich
THURSDAY	Caramel Bananas	Southern Slaw	Gremolata Swordfish Skewers
FRIDAY	Garlic Parmesan Grill Cheese Sandwiches	Grilled Asparagus and Honey Glazed Carrots	Greek Pork Skewers
SATURDAY	Blackberry Pie	Cheesy Ham and Pineapple Sandwich	Halibut Fillets with Spinach and Olives
SUNDAY	Ice Cream Bread	Healthy Broccoli	Ranch Chicken Burger Patties

CONCLUSION

Gas grills are becoming more popular because people are finding them safer, more reliable, and easier to use than charcoal grills. Gas grills can also be stored away during the winter, which is a huge benefit for anyone who lives in an area that has harsh winters. Some disadvantages could be that gas grills have a higher upfront cost, they usually have less cooking space than charcoal grills because of the gas tank being stored inside or on one side of it, and propane tanks need to be refilled, which could get costly if you grill frequently.

Gas grills are a great alternative to charcoal. If you live in an area where there is no source of charcoal or if you don't have space for a charcoal grill for storage reasons, a gas grill is an extremely great option. Propane tanks are easy to transport and can be refilled at most hardware stores. With a gas grill, you don't have the high cost of maintaining a charcoal grill and the added benefit of being able to cook food faster than with a charcoal grill. Gas grills have been extremely popular over the past decade as they have become more affordable and as people's concerns for safety have increased. Gas grills are a safe and efficient choice for anyone who cares about their health and wants to cook food on an efficient and easy-to-use grill.

Many people love the idea of grilling outside with friends and family during the summer. However, if you live in an area with harsh winters, then having a grill that won't use up your storage space through the winter is crucial. Also, not all areas have easily accessible charcoal. Furthermore, charcoal grills are more prone to burning yourself on the grill because it is so hot. Gas grills are much safer to use: one simple adjustment of a knob can disable the gas so you won't have to worry about it being lit when you are done cooking or closing up the shop for the night.

Index by Ingredients